Cakes

THE AUSTRALIAN
Women's Weekly

Cakes

acp
books

CONTENTS

introduction 6

butter cakes 8

chocolate cakes 54

sponge cakes 100

fruit cakes 138

syrup cakes 206

cupcakes 236

friands, muffins
    & scones 284

dessert cakes 336

glossary 386

index 392

conversion chart 399

Successful cake making is all about the careful weighing and measuring of ingredients, correct mixing, baking and cooling. Here are some extra tips related to the three most popular methods of cake-making:

Butter cakes If a recipe uses a method where the butter, sugar and eggs are beaten together (most butter-based cakes) the butter and eggs should be at room temperature. Soften the butter slightly if you must, but don't melt it, or the results could be disappointing.

Sponge cakes are made by beating eggs and sugar together until the sugar is dissolved, every sugar grain must be dissolved before moving onto the next step – the trickiest – and that's folding in the triple-sifted (for aeration) dry ingredients and any liquid. Use a slotted spoon, whisk, spatula or your hand with your fingers spread out like a rake, to pull the dry ingredients and liquid gently through the egg mixture.

One-bowl There are three one-bowl methods of cake making. First, rubbing the butter into the dry ingredients before adding the remaining ingredients – mostly used for heavier loaves – barely stir the ingredients together using a fork or slotted spoon. Secondly, melting the butter with other ingredients, cooling it to the correct temperature – warm or cold – before stirring in the remaining ingredients. Last, the quick-mix method where all the ingredients are mixed in a bowl using an electric mixer. The butter and eggs need to be at room temperature, the mixing should start using a low speed, gradually increasing to medium, the mixture will change to a paler colour when it's ready.

Follow our Triple Tested® recipes to the letter and you'll soon become famous for your cakes.

BUTTER CAKES

caramel butter cake

125g butter, softened
1 teaspoon vanilla extract
1 cup (220g) firmly packed brown sugar
2 eggs
1 tablespoon golden syrup
1 cup (150g) plain flour
½ cup (75g) self-raising flour
1 teaspoon ground cinnamon
½ cup (125ml) milk
caramel icing
1 cup (220g) firmly packed brown sugar
60g butter
2 tablespoons milk
¾ cup (120g) icing sugar
2 teaspoons milk, extra

1 Preheat oven to 180°C/160°C fan-forced. Grease deep 20cm-round cake pan; line base with baking paper.
2 Beat butter, extract and sugar in small bowl with electric mixer until light and fluffy. Beat in eggs and golden syrup. Stir in sifted flours and spices and milk.
3 Spread mixture into pan; bake about 50 minutes. Stand cake in pan 5 minutes; turn, top-side up, onto wire rack to cool.
4 Meanwhile, make caramel icing. Spread icing on top of cold cake before serving.
caramel icing Stir brown sugar, butter and milk in saucepan constantly, over heat without boiling until sugar dissolves. Bring to the boil. Reduce heat; simmer, uncovered, for 3 minutes without stirring; stir in sifted icing sugar. Stir in extra milk until icing is of a spreadable consistency.

prep + cook time 1 hour 15 minutes **serves** 10

basic butter cake

250g butter, softened
1 teaspoon vanilla extract
1¼ cups (275g) caster sugar
3 eggs
2¼ cups (335g) self-raising flour
¾ cup (180ml) milk

1 Preheat oven to 180°C/160°C fan-forced. Grease deep 20cm-square or 22cm-round cake pan; line base and side(s) with baking paper.
2 Beat butter, extract and sugar in medium bowl with electric mixer until light and fluffy. Beat in eggs, one at a time. Stir in sifted flour and milk, in two batches.
3 Spread mixture into pan; bake about 1 hour. Stand cake in pan 5 minutes; turn, top-side up, onto wire rack to cool.

prep + cook time 1 hour 30 minutes **serves** 12

orange macaroon cake

125g butter, softened
2 teaspoons grated orange rind
¾ cup (165g) caster sugar
2 egg yolks
2 cups (300g) self-raising flour
¾ cup (180ml) milk
macaroon topping
2 egg whites
2 tablespoons caster sugar
½ teaspoon vanilla extract
½ cup (45g) desiccated coconut

1 Preheat oven to 180°C/160°C fan-forced. Grease 20cm x 30cm lamington pan; line base with baking paper.
2 Make macaroon topping.
3 Beat butter, rind, sugar and egg yolks in medium bowl with electric mixer until light and fluffy. Stir in flour and milk, in two batches. Spread mixture into pan; spread with topping.
4 Bake cake about 30 minutes. Stand cake in pan 5 minutes; turn, top-side up, onto wire rack to cool.
macaroon topping Beat egg whites in small bowl with electric mixer until soft peaks form; gradually add sugar, beating until dissolved. Stir in extract and coconut.

prep + cook time 55 minutes **serves** 16

lemon and apricot cake

180g butter, softened
1 tablespoon finely grated lemon rind
1¼ cups (275g) caster sugar
4 eggs
½ cup (125g) coarsely chopped glacé apricots
¼ cup (45g) finely chopped glacé ginger
¾ cup (180g) sour cream
2 cups (300g) plain flour
½ teaspoon bicarbonate of soda

1 Preheat oven to 180°C/160°C fan-forced. Grease 20cm baba pan; sprinkle with flour, shake out excess flour.
2 Beat butter, rind and sugar in small bowl with electric mixer until light and fluffy. Beat in eggs, one at a time. Fold in apricots, ginger and sour cream, then sifted flour and soda.
3 Spread mixture into pan; bake about 1 hour. Stand cake in pan 10 minutes; turn, top-side up, onto wire rack to cool. Serve dusted with icing sugar, if you like.

prep + cook time 1 hour 25 minutes **serves** 8

pecan sour cream cake

250g butter, softened
1 teaspoon vanilla extract
¾ cup (165g) caster sugar
2 eggs
300g sour cream
1½ cups (225g) plain flour
½ cup (75g) self-raising flour
1 teaspoon bicarbonate of soda
½ cup (60g) finely chopped pecans
2 tablespoons brown sugar
½ teaspoon ground cinnamon

1 Preheat oven to 180°C/160°C fan-forced. Grease deep 23cm-round cake pan; line base with baking paper.
2 Beat butter, extract and caster sugar in small bowl with electric mixer until light and fluffy. Beat in eggs, one at a time. Stir in sour cream and sifted flours and soda.
3 Spread half the cake mixture into pan; sprinkle with half the combined nuts, brown sugar and cinnamon. Spread with remaining cake mixture; sprinkle with remaining pecan mixture.
4 Bake cake about 1 hour. Stand cake in pan 5 minutes; turn, top-side up, onto wire rack to cool.

prep + cook time 1 hour 15 minutes **serves** 10

orange cake

150g butter, softened
1 tablespoon finely grated orange rind
⅔ cup (150g) caster sugar
3 eggs
1½ cups (225g) self-raising flour
¼ cup (60ml) milk
orange icing
¾ cup (120g) icing sugar
1½ tablespoons orange juice

1 Preheat oven to 180°C/160°C fan-forced. Grease deep 20cm-round cake pan.
2 Beat butter, rind, sugar, eggs, flour and milk in medium bowl with electric mixer at low speed until just combined. Increase speed to medium, beat about 3 minutes or until mixture is smooth.
3 Spread mixture into pan; bake about 40 minutes. Stand cake in pan 5 minutes; turn, top-side up, onto wire rack to cool.
4 Make orange icing. Spread icing over top of cake.
orange icing Stir ingredients in small bowl until smooth.

prep + cook time 50 minutes **serves** 12

orange marmalade cake

125g butter
2 teaspoons finely grated orange rind
½ cup (110g) caster sugar
2 eggs
2 tablespoons orange marmalade
⅓ cup (55g) dried mixed peel
½ cup (45g) desiccated coconut
1½ cups (225g) self-raising flour
½ cup (125ml) milk

1 Preheat oven to 180°C/160°C fan-forced. Grease 14cm x 21cm loaf pan; line base and 2 long sides with a strip of baking paper, extending paper 2cm above edge of pan.
2 Beat butter, rind and sugar in small bowl with electric mixer until light and fluffy. Beat in eggs. Transfer mixture to large bowl; stir in marmalade and peel, then coconut, flour and milk.
3 Spread mixture into pan; bake about 1 hour. Stand 5 minutes; turn, top-side up, onto wire rack to cool.

prep + cook time 1 hour 15 minutes **serves** 10

cinnamon teacake

60g butter, softened
1 teaspoon vanilla extract
⅔ cup (150g) caster sugar
1 egg
1 cup (150g) self-raising flour
⅓ cup (80ml) milk
10g butter, melted, extra
1 teaspoon ground cinnamon
1 tablespoon caster sugar, extra

1 Preheat oven to 180°C/160°C fan-forced. Grease deep 20cm-round cake pan; line base with baking paper.
2 Beat butter, extract, sugar and egg in small bowl with electric mixer until light and fluffy, this will take about 10 minutes. Stir in sifted flour and milk.
3 Spread mixture into pan; bake about 30 minutes. Turn cake onto wire rack then turn top-side up; brush top with extra butter, sprinkle with combined cinnamon and extra sugar. Serve warm with butter, if you like.

prep + cook time 45 minutes **serves** 10

almond butter cake

250g butter, softened
1 teaspoon almond essence
1 cup (220g) caster sugar
4 eggs
1 cup (150g) self-raising flour
½ cup (75g) plain flour
¾ cup (90g) ground almonds

1 Preheat oven to 180°C/160°C fan-forced. Grease deep 20cm-square cake pan; line base and two opposite sides with baking paper, extending paper 5cm over edges.
2 Beat butter, essence and sugar in medium bowl with electric mixer until light and fluffy. Beat in eggs, one at a time. Fold in sifted flours and ground almonds, in two batches.
3 Spread mixture into pan; bake for 30 minutes. Reduce oven to 160°C/140°C fan-forced; bake a further 30 minutes. Stand cake in pan 5 minutes; turn, top-side up, onto wire rack to cool. Serve dusted with icing sugar and toasted flaked almonds, if you like.

prep + cook time 1 hour 20 minutes **serves** 10

madeira cake

180g butter, softened
2 teaspoons finely grated lemon rind
⅔ cup (150g) caster sugar
3 eggs
¾ cup (110g) plain flour
¾ cup (110g) self-raising flour
⅓ cup (55g) mixed peel
¼ cup (35g) slivered almonds

1 Preheat oven to 160°C/140°C fan-forced. Grease deep 20cm-round cake pan; line base with paper.
2 Beat butter, rind and sugar in small bowl with electric mixer until light and fluffy. Beat in eggs, one at a time. Transfer mixture to large bowl; stir in sifted flours.
3 Spread mixture into pan; bake 20 minutes. Remove cake from oven; sprinkle with peel and nuts. Return to oven; bake about 40 minutes. Stand cake in pan 5 minutes; turn, top-side up, onto wire rack to cool.

prep + cook time 1 hour 15 minutes **serves** 12

pumpkin date cake

You need to cook 200g pumpkin to get the required amount of mashed pumpkin.

250g butter, softened
1 tablespoon grated orange rind
¾ cup (165g) caster sugar
2 eggs
2 cups (300g) self-raising flour
½ cup (125ml) milk
1 cup (140g) finely chopped dates
½ cup (40g) desiccated coconut
½ cup cold mashed pumpkin

1 Preheat oven to 160°C/140°C fan-forced. Grease deep 20cm-round cake pan; line base with baking paper.
2 Beat butter, rind and sugar in small bowl with electric mixer until light and fluffy. Beat in eggs, one at a time. Transfer mixture to large bowl; stir in sifted flour and milk, then dates, coconut and pumpkin.
3 Spread mixture into pan; bake about 1¼ hours. Stand cake in pan 5 minutes; turn, top-side up, onto wire rack to cool. Serve dusted with sifted icing sugar.

prep + cook time 1 hour 30 minutes **serves** 10

marble cake

250g butter, softened
1 teaspoon vanilla extract
1¼ cups (275g) caster sugar
3 eggs
2¼ cups (335g) self-raising flour
¾ cup (180ml) milk
pink food colouring
2 tablespoons cocoa powder
2 tablespoons milk, extra
butter frosting
90g butter, softened
1 cup (160g) icing sugar
1 tablespoon milk

1 Preheat oven to 180°C/160°C fan-forced. Grease deep 22cm-round or 20cm-square cake pan; line base with baking paper.
2 Beat butter, extract and sugar in medium bowl with electric mixer until light and fluffy. Beat in eggs, one at a time. Stir in sifted flour and milk, in two batches.
3 Divide mixture among three bowls; tint one mixture pink. Blend sifted cocoa with extra milk in cup; stir into second mixture. leave remaining mixture plain. Drop alternate spoonfuls of mixtures into pan. Pull a skewer backwards and forwards through cake mixture.
4 Bake cake about 1 hour. Stand cake in pan 5 minutes; turn, top-side up, onto wire rack to cool.
5 Make butter frosting. Spread frosting over top and side of cake.
butter frosting Beat butter in small bowl with electric mixer until light and fluffy; beat in sifted icing sugar and milk, in two batches.

prep + cook time 1 hour 40 minutes (+ cooling) **serves** 12

cream cheese lemon cake

125g butter, chopped
125g cream cheese, chopped
3 teaspoons finely grated lemon rind
1 cup (220g) caster sugar
2 eggs
¾ cup (110g) self-raising flour
½ cup (75g) plain flour
glacé icing
1 cup (160g) icing sugar
10g butter, melted
2 tablespoons hot water approximately
½ teaspoon finely grated lemon rind

1 Preheat oven to 180°C/160°C fan-forced. Grease 20cm baba pan or grease and line deep 20cm-round cake pan with baking paper.
2 Beat ingredients in medium bowl on low speed with electric mixer until combined. Increase speed to medium; beat about 3 minutes or until mixture is smooth and pale in colour.
3 Spread mixture into pan; bake about 55 minutes. Stand cake in pan 5 minutes; turn, top-side up, onto wire rack to cool.
4 Meanwhile, make glacé icing. Spoon icing over cold cake.
glacé icing Sift icing sugar into small heatproof bowl; stir in butter and enough of the water to make a firm paste. Stand bowl over small saucepan of simmering water; stir icing until spreadable. Stir in rind.

prep + cook time 1 hour 15 minutes **serves** 10

pound cake

250g butter, softened
1 cup (220g) caster sugar
1 teaspoon vanilla extract
4 eggs
½ cup (75g) self-raising flour
1 cup (150g) plain flour

1 Preheat oven to 180°C/160°C fan-forced. Grease deep 20cm-round cake pan; line base with baking paper.
2 Beat butter, sugar and extract in small bowl with electric mixer until light and fluffy. Beat in eggs, one at a time. Transfer mixture to large bowl; fold in sifted flours in two batches.
3 Spread mixture into pan; bake about 1 hour. Stand cake in pan 5 minutes; turn, top-side up, onto wire rack to cool. If you like, dust cake with sifted icing sugar and serve with whipped cream and strawberries.

prep + cook time 1 hour 20 minutes **serves** 12

pecan and date ripple cake

125g butter, softened
1 teaspoon vanilla extract
1 cup (220g) caster sugar
2 eggs
1 cup (150g) plain flour
1 cup (150g) self-raising flour
300ml sour cream
½ cup (80g) seeded chopped dates
pecan topping
½ cup (60g) chopped pecans
2 tablespoons demerara sugar
1 teaspoon ground cinnamon

1 Preheat oven to 180°C/160°C fan-forced. Grease deep 20cm-round cake pan; line base with baking paper.
2 Make pecan topping.
3 Beat butter, extract and sugar in small bowl with electric mixer until light and fluffy. Beat in eggs. Transfer mixture to large bowl; stir in sifted flours, sour cream, then dates.
4 Spread half the cake mixture into pan; sprinkle with half the pecan topping. Spread with remaining cake mixture; sprinkle with remaining topping, press down lightly.
5 Bake cake about 1 hour. Stand cake in pan 5 minutes; turn, top-side up, onto wire rack to cool.
pecan topping Combine ingredients in small bowl.

prep + cook time 1 hour 15 minutes **serves** 12

coconut cake

125g butter, softened
½ teaspoon coconut essence
1 cup (220g) caster sugar
2 eggs
½ cup (40g) desiccated coconut
1½ cups (225g) self-raising flour
1¼ cups (300g) sour cream
⅓ cup (80ml) milk
coconut ice frosting
2 cups (320g) icing sugar
1⅓ cups (100g) desiccated coconut
2 egg whites, beaten lightly
pink food colouring

1 Preheat oven to 180°C/160°C fan-forced. Grease deep 23cm-square cake pan; line with baking paper.
2 Beat butter, essence and sugar in small bowl with electric mixer until light and fluffy. Beat in eggs, one at a time. Transfer mixture to large bowl; stir in coconut, sifted flour, sour cream and milk, in two batches.
3 Spread mixture into pan; bake about 40 minutes. Stand cake in pan 5 minutes; turn, top-side up, onto wire rack to cool.
4 Meanwhile, make coconut ice frosting. Drop alternate spoonfuls of white and pink frosting onto cake; marble over top of cake.
coconut ice frosting Sift icing sugar into medium bowl; stir in coconut and egg white. Place half the mixture in small bowl; tint with pink colouring.

prep + cook time 1 hour 5 minutes **serves** 20

kisses

125g butter, softened
½ cup (110g) caster sugar
1 egg
⅓ cup (50g) plain flour
¼ cup (35g) self-raising flour
⅔ cup (100g) cornflour
¼ cup (30g) custard powder
vienna cream
60g butter, softened
¾ cup (120g) icing sugar
2 teaspoons milk

1 Preheat oven to 180°C/160°C fan-forced. Grease two oven trays.
2 Beat butter and sugar in small bowl with electric mixer until smooth and creamy; beat in egg. Stir in sifted dry ingredients in two batches.
3 Spoon mixture into piping bag fitted with 1cm tube. Pipe 3cm-diameter rounds of mixture, about 3cm apart, onto trays.
4 Bake cakes about 10 minutes or until browned lightly. Loosen cakes; cool on trays.
5 Meanwhile, make vienna cream.
6 Sandwich cold cakes with vienna cream; dust with a little extra sifted icing sugar, if desired.
vienna cream Beat butter until as white as possible. Gradually beat in half the sifted icing sugar; beat in milk. Gradually beat in remaining icing sugar.

prep + cook time 40 minutes **makes** about 40

passionfruit buttermilk cake

You need about 6 passionfruit to get the required amount of pulp.

250g butter, softened
1 cup (220g) caster sugar
3 eggs, separated
2 cups (300g) self-raising flour
¾ cup (180ml) buttermilk
¼ cup (60ml) passionfruit pulp
passionfruit icing
1½ cups (240g) icing sugar
¼ cup (60ml) passionfruit pulp, approximately

1 Preheat oven to 180°C/160°C fan-forced. Grease 24cm bundt tin or 21cm baba cake pan; sprinkle with flour, shake out excess flour.
2 Beat butter and sugar in small bowl with electric mixer until light and fluffy. Beat in egg yolks, one at a time. Transfer mixture to large bowl; stir in sifted flour and buttermilk, in two batches. Stir in passionfruit pulp.
3 Beat egg whites in small bowl with electric mixer until soft peaks form. Fold into cake mixture, in two batches.
4 Spread mixture into tin; bake about 40 minutes. Stand cake 5 minutes; turn, top-side up, onto wire rack to cool.
5 Meanwhile, make passionfruit icing. Drizzle icing over cold cake.
passionfruit icing Sift icing sugar into heatproof bowl; stir in enough passionfruit pulp to form a firm paste. Stand bowl over small saucepan of simmering water; stir icing until of a pouring consistency (do not overheat).

prep + cook time 1 hour 10 minutes (+ cooling) **serves** 8

pear and almond cake with passionfruit glaze

You need about 4 passionfruit to get the required amount of pulp.

185g butter, softened
½ cup (110g) caster sugar
3 eggs
1½ cups (175g) ground almonds
¼ cup (35g) plain flour
420g can pear halves in natural juice, drained
passionfruit glaze
⅓ cup (80ml) passionfruit pulp
⅓ cup (80ml) light corn syrup
1 tablespoon caster sugar

1 Preheat oven to 160°C/140°C fan-forced. Grease 22cm springform tin; line base and side with baking paper.
2 Beat butter and sugar in medium bowl with electric mixer until light and fluffy. Beat in eggs, one at a time. Stir in ground almonds and flour.
3 Spread mixture into tin; top with pear halves, cut-side down.
4 Bake cake about 50 minutes. Stand cake in tin 5 minutes; transfer to serving plate.
5 Meanwhile, make passionfruit glaze. Pour glaze over cake while still warm.
passionfruit glaze Stir ingredients in small saucepan over heat, without boiling, until sugar dissolves. Bring to the boil. Reduce heat; simmer, uncovered, without stirring, 2 minutes or until thickened slightly. Cool.

prep + cook time 1 hour 25 minutes (+ cooling) **serves** 10

coffee caramel cakes

2 tablespoons instant coffee granules
1 tablespoon boiling water
125g butter, softened
²⁄₃ cup (150g) firmly packed brown sugar
2 eggs
2 cups (300g) self-raising flour
½ cup (125ml) milk
18 (130g) jersey caramels, halved

1 Preheat oven to 180°C/160°C fan-forced. Grease 12-hole (⅓-cup/
80ml) muffin pan.
2 Dissolve coffee in the water. Beat butter and sugar in small bowl with
electric mixer until light and fluffy. Add coffee mixture, then beat in eggs,
one at a time. Transfer mixture to large bowl; stir in sifted flour and milk.
3 Spoon mixture into pan holes; gently push 3 caramel halves into centre
of each cake and cover with batter.
4 Bake cakes about 20 minutes. Cool cakes in pan 5 minutes; turn,
top-side up, onto wire racks to cool.

prep + cook time 35 minutes (+ cooling) **makes** 12

coffee walnut streusel cake

1 tablespoon instant coffee granules
¼ cup (60ml) boiling water
125g butter, softened
1 cup (220g) caster sugar
1 teaspoon vanilla extract
2 eggs
⅔ cup (160g) sour cream
1¼ cups (185g) plain flour
¼ cup (35g) self-raising flour
¼ teaspoon bicarbonate of soda
½ cup (55g) coarsely chopped roasted walnuts
walnut streusel
⅔ cup (100g) self-raising flour
⅔ cup (150g) firmly packed brown sugar
100g cold butter, chopped
½ cup (55g) coarsely chopped roasted walnuts

1 Preheat oven to 180°C/160°C fan-forced. Grease deep 22cm-round cake pan; line base with baking paper.
2 Combine coffee and water in small bowl; stir until coffee dissolves. Cool 5 minutes.
3 Make walnut streusel.
4 Beat butter, sugar and extract in medium bowl with electric mixer until light and fluffy. Beat in eggs, one at a time. Stir in sour cream and sifted flours and soda, in two batches. Stir in coffee mixture.
5 Spread mixture into pan; sprinkle walnut streusel over cake mixture, sprinkle walnuts over streusel.
6 Bake cake about 30 minutes. Stand cake in pan 5 minutes; turn, top-side up, onto wire rack to cool.
walnut streusel Combine flour and sugar in medium bowl; rub in butter, using fingertips, until mixture resembles coarse breadcrumbs. Stir in the walnuts.

prep + cook time 1 hour **serves** 12

butterfly cakes

125g butter, softened
1 teaspoon vanilla extract
⅔ cup (150g) caster sugar
3 eggs
1½ cups (225g) self-raising flour
¼ cup (60ml) milk
½ cup (160g) jam
300ml thickened cream, whipped

1 Preheat oven to 180°C/160°C fan-forced. Line two 12-hole
(2-tablespoon/40ml) deep flat-based patty pans with paper cases.
2 Beat butter, extract, sugar, eggs, sifted flour and milk in small bowl
on low speed with electric mixer until ingredients are just combined.
Increase speed to medium; beat about 3 minutes or until mixture is
smooth and pale in colour.
3 Drop slightly rounded tablespoons of mixture into paper cases.
Bake about 20 minutes. Stand cakes in pans 5 minutes before turning,
top-side up, onto wire racks to cool.
4 Using sharp pointed vegetable knife, cut a circle from the top of each
cake; cut circle in half to make two "wings". Fill cavities with jam and
whipped cream. Place wings in position on top of cakes. Dust with a
little sifted icing sugar before serving, if you like.

prep + cook time 50 minutes **makes** 24

CHOCOLATE
CAKES

chocolate orange fudge cake

125g butter, chopped coarsely
250g dark eating chocolate, chopped coarsely
⅔ cup (100g) self-raising flour
⅔ cup (150g) caster sugar
3 eggs
2 teaspoons finely grated orange rind
¼ cup (60ml) orange juice
2 tablespoons orange-flavoured liqueur
choc orange ganache
200g dark eating chocolate, chopped
2 teaspoons finely grated orange rind
⅔ cup (160ml) cream

1 Preheat oven to 180°C/160°C fan-forced. Grease deep 20cm-round cake pan; line base and side with baking paper.
2 Stir butter and chocolate in medium saucepan over low heat until smooth. Transfer mixture to large bowl; cool 10 minutes.
3 Add sifted flour, sugar, eggs, rind, juice and liqueur to chocolate mixture; beat on low speed with electric mixer until ingredients are combined. Increase speed to medium; beat about 2 minutes or until mixture is smooth and paler in colour.
4 Pour mixture into pan; bake about 1 hour. Stand cake in pan 5 minutes; turn, top-side up, onto wire rack to cool.
5 Meanwhile, make choc orange ganache. Spread cake with ganache. Serve with whipped cream, if you like.
choc orange ganache Combine chocolate and rind in medium bowl. Bring cream to the boil in small saucepan. Add cream to chocolate mixture; stir until smooth. Stand 15 minutes or until ganache is spreadable.

prep + cook time 1 hour 15 minutes (+ standing) **serves** 10
tip We used Cointreau for this recipe but you can use any orange-flavoured liqueur you like.

sour cream chocolate cake

125g butter, softened
1 cup (220g) firmly packed brown sugar
2 eggs
2/3 cup (160ml) milk
1 cup (240g) sour cream
2 cups (300g) self-raising flour
2/3 cup (70g) cocoa powder
sour cream ganache
2/3 cup (160g) sour cream
200g dark eating chocolate, chopped coarsely

1 Preheat oven to 180°C/160°C fan-forced. Grease deep 23cm-round cake pan; line base and side with baking paper.
2 Beat butter and sugar in small bowl with electric mixer until light and fluffy. Beat in eggs, one at a time. Transfer mixture to large bowl; stir in combined milk and sour cream and sifted dry ingredients, in two batches.
3 Spread mixture into pan; tap pan on bench to remove any large air pockets. Bake about 50 minutes. Stand cake in pan 5 minutes; turn, top-side up, onto wire rack to cool.
4 Meanwhile, make sour cream ganache.
5 Split cake in half; sandwich with half the ganache. Spread top of cake with remaining ganache.

sour cream ganache Stir ingredients in small saucepan over low heat until smooth. Cool about 45 minutes or until spreadable.

prep + cook time 1 hour 15 minutes (+ cooling) **serves** 10

sacher torte

150g dark eating chocolate,
  chopped
1 tablespoon water
150g butter, softened
½ cup (110g) caster sugar
3 eggs, separated
1 cup (150g) plain flour
2 tablespoons caster sugar, extra
1 cup (320g) apricot jam,
  warmed, strained

chocolate icing
125g dark eating chocolate,
  chopped
125g butter, softened

1 Preheat oven to 180°C/160°C fan-forced. Grease deep 22cm-round cake pan; line base with baking paper.

2 Melt chocolate in small heatproof bowl over small saucepan of simmering water (do not allow water to touch base of bowl); stir in the water. Cool to room temperature.

3 Beat butter and sugar in small bowl with electric mixer until light and fluffy. Beat in egg yolks one at a time until combined. Transfer mixture to large bowl; stir in chocolate mixture, then sifted flour.

4 Beat egg whites in small bowl until soft peaks form, gradually beat in extra sugar until dissolved between each addition; fold into chocolate mixture.

5 Spread mixture into pan; bake about 30 minutes. Stand cake in pan 5 minutes; turn onto wire rack to cool, leaving cake upside down.

6 Meanwhile, make chocolate icing.

7 Split cold cake in half; place one half, cut-side up, on serving plate. Brush half the warmed jam over cake half, top with remaining cake half. Brush cake all over with remaining jam. Stand about 1 hour at room temperature or until jam has set. Spread top and side of cake with icing; stand at room temperature until icing has set. Serve with berries, if you like.

chocolate icing Melt chocolate and butter in small heatproof bowl over small saucepan of simmering water (do not allow water to touch base of bowl). Cool at room temperature until spreadable, stirring occasionally; this can take up to 2 hours.

prep + cook time 1 hour 10 minutes (+ standing & cooling) **serves** 10
tip This icing is also suitable for piping.

gluten-free chocolate cakes

This recipe is gluten-free, yeast-free and wheat-free.

200g butter, softened
2¼ cups (300g) gluten-free self-raising flour
¼ cup (25g) cocoa powder
1 cup (220g) caster sugar
¾ cup (180ml) milk
2 eggs
2 egg whites
chocolate icing
1 cup (160g) pure icing sugar
1 tablespoon cocoa powder
2 tablespoons water

1 Preheat oven to 180°C/160°C fan-forced. Line two 12-hole (⅓-cup/ 80ml) muffin pans with paper cases.
2 Beat butter in large bowl with electric mixer until pale. Beat sifted flour, cocoa and ¼ cup of the caster sugar alternately with milk into butter, in two batches, until combined.
3 Beat eggs and egg whites in small bowl with electric mixer until thick and creamy. Gradually add remaining caster sugar, one tablespoon at a time, beating until sugar dissolves between additions. Gradually beat egg mixture into flour mixture until combined.
4 Spoon 2½ tablespoons mixture into each paper case; bake about 20 minutes. Turn, top-side-up, onto wire rack to cool.
5 Meanwhile, make chocolate icing. Spread cold cakes with icing.
chocolate icing Sift sugar and cocoa into small bowl; stir in water until smooth.

prep + cook time 40 minutes (+ cooling) **makes** 24

family chocolate cake

2 cups (500ml) water
3 cups (660g) caster sugar
250g butter, chopped
⅓ cup (35g) cocoa powder
1 teaspoon bicarbonate of soda
3 cups (450g) self-raising flour
4 eggs
fudge frosting
90g butter
⅓ cup (80ml) water
½ cup (110g) caster sugar
1½ cups (240g) icing sugar
⅓ cup (35g) cocoa powder

1 Preheat oven to 180°C/160°C fan-forced. Grease deep 26.5cm x 33cm (3.5-litre/14-cup) baking dish; line base with baking paper.
2 Stir the water, sugar, butter and sifted cocoa and soda in medium saucepan over heat, without boiling, until sugar dissolves; bring to the boil. Reduce heat; simmer, uncovered, 5 minutes. Transfer mixture to large bowl; cool to room temperature.
3 Add flour and eggs to bowl; beat with electric mixer until mixture is smooth and pale in colour.
4 Pour mixture into dish; bake about 50 minutes. Stand cake in dish 10 minutes; turn, top-side up, onto wire rack to cool.
5 Meanwhile, make fudge frosting. Spread cold cake with frosting.
fudge frosting Stir butter, the water and caster sugar in small saucepan over low heat, without boiling, until sugar dissolves. Sift icing sugar and cocoa into small bowl then gradually stir in hot butter mixture. Cover; refrigerate about 20 minutes or until frosting thickens. Beat frosting with wooden spoon until it is spreadable.

prep + cook time 1 hour 10 minutes (+ cooling) **serves** 16

64

rum and raisin chocolate cake

¼ cup (60ml) dark rum
1 cup (180g) raisins, chopped finely
300g dark eating chocolate, chopped coarsely
150g butter, chopped coarsely
⅔ cup (150g) firmly packed brown sugar
⅔ cup (100g) self-raising flour
2 tablespoons cocoa powder
3 eggs, separated
2 teaspoons cocoa powder, extra

1 Preheat oven to 180°C/160°C fan-forced. Grease deep 23cm-round cake pan; line base and side with baking paper.
2 Warm rum in small saucepan, add raisins; stand 1 hour.
3 Stir chocolate and butter in small saucepan over low heat until smooth. Transfer to large bowl; cool 5 minutes. Stir in sugar, sifted flour and cocoa, egg yolks and raisin mixture.
4 Beat egg whites in small bowl with electric mixer until soft peaks form; fold into chocolate mixture, in two batches.
5 Pour mixture into pan; bake about 1 hour. Stand cake in pan 15 minutes; turn, top-side up, onto serving plate. Serve cake warm or cold dusted with extra sifted cocoa and with whipped cream, if you like.

prep + cook time 1 hour 15 minutes (+ standing) **serves** 12

chocolate raspberry brownies

150g butter, chopped coarsely
350g dark eating chocolate, chopped coarsely
1 cup (220g) caster sugar
2 eggs
1¼ cups (185g) plain flour
½ cup (75g) self-raising flour
200g fresh or frozen raspberries
2 teaspoons cocoa powder

1 Preheat oven to 180°C/160°C fan-forced. Grease deep 20cm-square cake pan; line base and sides with baking paper, extending paper 5cm over edges.
2 Stir butter and 200g of the chocolate in medium saucepan over low heat until smooth. Cool 10 minutes.
3 Stir sugar, eggs, sifted flours, raspberries and remaining chopped chocolate into chocolate mixture; spread into pan.
4 Bake brownies about 45 minutes. Cool in pan before cutting into 16 squares. Serve brownies dusted with sifted cocoa.

prep + cook time 1 hour 10 minutes **makes** 16 squares
tip If using frozen raspberries don't thaw them before adding to the mixture otherwise they'll bleed and won't retain their shape.

triple chocolate brownies

125g butter, chopped
200g dark eating chocolate, chopped
½ cup (110g) caster sugar
2 eggs
1¼ cups (185g) plain flour
150g white eating chocolate, chopped
100g milk eating chocolate, chopped

1 Preheat oven to 180°C/160°C fan-forced. Grease deep 19cm-square cake pan; line base with baking paper, extending paper 5cm over sides.
2 Stir butter and dark chocolate in medium saucepan over low heat until smooth. Cool 10 minutes.
3 Stir in sugar and eggs then sifted flour and white and milk chocolates. Spread mixture into pan.
4 Bake brownies about 35 minutes. Cool in pan before cutting into 16 squares.

prep + cook time 1 hour **makes** 16 squares

easy chocolate cake

125g butter, softened
1 teaspoon vanilla extract
1¼ cups (275g) caster sugar
2 eggs
1⅓ cups (200g) self-raising flour
½ cup (50g) cocoa powder
⅔ cup (160ml) water
chocolate icing
90g dark eating chocolate, chopped coarsely
30g butter
1 cup (160g) icing sugar
2 tablespoons hot water

1 Preheat oven to 180°C/160°C fan-forced. Grease deep 20cm-round cake pan; line with baking paper.
2 Beat butter, extract, sugar, eggs, sifted flour and cocoa, and the water in large bowl with electric mixer on low speed until ingredients are combined. Increase speed to medium; beat about 3 minutes or until mixture is smooth and paler in colour.
3 Spread mixture into pan; bake about 1 hour. Stand cake in pan 5 minutes; turn, top-side up, onto wire rack to cool.
4 Meanwhile, make chocolate icing. Spread cake with icing.
chocolate icing Melt chocolate and butter in small heatproof bowl over small saucepan of simmering water; gradually stir in sifted icing sugar and the hot water, stirring until icing is spreadable.

prep + cook time 1 hour 10 minutes (+ cooling) **serves** 20
tip This cake can be stored in an airtight container for up to 3 days.

mini chocolate yule logs

1 cup (150g) seeded dried dates
1 cup (190g) seeded prunes
1 cup (200g) dried figs
1 cup (140g) brazil nuts
2 eggs
½ cup (110g) firmly packed
    brown sugar
1 tablespoon dark rum
100g butter, melted

⅓ cup (50g) plain four
¼ cup (35g) self-raising flour
100g dark eating chocolate,
    melted
1 tablespoon icing sugar
chocolate ganache
200g dark eating chocolate,
    chopped coarsely
½ cup (125ml) cream

1 Preheat oven to 150°C/130°C fan-forced. Grease eight, cleaned cans (see tip); line with baking paper.
2 Chop fruit and nuts finely; combine in large bowl.
3 Beat eggs and sugar in small bowl with electric mixer until thick and creamy. Add rum, butter and sifted flours; beat until combined. Stir egg mixture into fruit mixture. Push mixture firmly into cans; place on oven tray.
4 Bake cakes about 30 minutes. Turn top-side up onto wire rack to cool.
5 Meanwhile, make chocolate ganache.
6 Line tray with baking paper; spread melted chocolate into 26cm square. Refrigerate until set.
7 Cut four of the cakes in half crossways. Sandwich one large cake and one half cake, end-to-end, together with ganache. Repeat with remaining large cakes and three of the halves of remaining cake to make four logs.
8 Trim bottom corner from each of the remaining cake halves. Attach to sides of long cakes with ganache.
9 Place logs on boards or plates; spread all over with ganache. Break chocolate into small pieces, gently push into ganache. Refrigerate until set. Serve dusted with sifted icing sugar.
chocolate ganache Stir ingredients in small bowl over small saucepan of simmering water until smooth. Refrigerate about 30 minutes, stirring occasionally, until spreadable.

prep + cook time 1 hour 15 minutes (+ cooling & refrigeration) **makes** 4
tip We baked these cakes in eight 170g passionfruit pulp cans (5.5cm x 8.5cm). Open the cans with an opener that removes the rims from cans (ring-pull cans are not suitable). Freeze pulp for another use. Remove and discard the paper label from cans, then wash and dry the cans well.

fig and muscat brownie

½ cup (100g) finely chopped dried figs
¼ cup (60ml) muscat
125g butter, chopped coarsely
200g dark eating chocolate, chopped coarsely
⅔ cup (150g) caster sugar
2 eggs, beaten lightly
1¼ cups (185g) plain flour
150g dark eating chocolate, chopped coarsely, extra
1 tablespoon cocoa powder

1 Combine figs and muscat in small bowl; stand 20 minutes.
2 Preheat oven to 180°C/160°C fan-forced. Grease deep 19cm-square cake pan; line base and sides with baking paper, extending paper 5cm over sides.
3 Stir butter and chocolate in medium saucepan over low heat until smooth. Cool 10 minutes.
4 Stir in sugar and eggs then sifted flour, extra chocolate and fig mixture. Spread mixture into pan.
5 Bake brownies about 30 minutes. Cool in pan. Dust brownies with sifted cocoa then cut into 36 squares.

prep + cook time 50 minutes **makes** 36

white christmas mud cakes

125g butter, chopped coarsely
125g white eating chocolate,
  chopped coarsely
²⁄₃ cup (150g) caster sugar
²⁄₃ cup (160ml) milk
¾ cup (105g) plain flour
¼ cup (35g) self-raising flour
2 eggs
2 tablespoons orange-flavoured
  liqueur
60g white eating chocolate
  melted, extra
1 tablespoon icing sugar

white christmas
120g white eating chocolate,
  chopped coarsely
2 teaspoons vegetable oil
¾ cup (30g) rice bubbles
100g marshmallows with toasted
  coconut, chopped finely
¼ cup (35g) coarsely chopped
  unsalted pistachios
¼ cup (35g) coarsely chopped
  dried cranberries
¼ cup (60g) finely chopped
  glacé peaches

1 Preheat oven to 160°C/140°C fan-forced. Grease eight ¾-cup (180ml) pudding moulds.

2 Stir butter, chocolate, caster sugar and milk in medium saucepan over low heat until smooth. Transfer to medium bowl; cool 10 minutes. Whisk in sifted flours, then eggs.

3 Spoon mixture into moulds; place on oven tray. Bake about 30 minutes; drizzle cakes with liqueur. Turn hot cakes, still in their moulds, upside down onto baking-paper-lined tray; stand overnight.

4 Cut four 20cm circles from baking paper; cut circles in half. Roll each half into a tight cone. Staple or tape cones to hold their shape.

5 Make white christmas. Push spoonfuls of white christmas firmly into cones. Stand each cone upright in a tall narrow glass. Refrigerate cones about 1 hour or until set.

6 Remove cakes from moulds. Trim tops of cakes to make flat; turn upside down onto tray. Remove paper from white christmas cones; secure cones to each cake with a little of the extra chocolate. Refrigerate 10 minutes. Serve mud cakes dusted with sifted icing sugar.

white christmas Stir chocolate and oil in small saucepan over low heat until smooth. Combine rice bubbles, marshmallow, nuts and fruit in medium bowl; stir in melted chocolate mixture.

prep + cook time 1 hour 25 minutes (+ standing & refrigeration) **makes** 8
tip We used Cointreau for this recipe but you can use any orange-flavoured liqueur you like.

chocolate velvet cake

125g butter, softened
1 cup (220g) firmly packed brown sugar
½ cup (110g) caster sugar
3 eggs
2 cups (300g) plain flour
⅓ cup (35g) cocoa powder
1 teaspoon bicarbonate of soda
⅔ cup (160g) sour cream
½ cup (125ml) water
chocolate glaze
100g dark eating chocolate, chopped coarsely
60g butter, chopped coarsely
½ cup (80g) icing sugar
¼ cup (60g) sour cream

1 Preheat oven to 180°C/160°C fan-forced. Grease deep 22cm x 32cm rectangular cake pan; line base and sides with baking paper, extending paper 5cm over sides.
2 Beat ingredients in large bowl with electric mixer on low speed until ingredients are combined. Increase speed to medium; beat about 3 minutes or until mixture is smooth and paler in colour.
3 Spread mixture into pan; bake about 45 minutes. Stand cake in pan 10 minutes; turn, top-side up, onto wire rack to cool.
4 Meanwhile, make chocolate glaze. Spread cold cake with chocolate glaze. Serve with whipped cream, if you like.
chocolate glaze Stir ingredients in small saucepan over low heat until smooth; cook, stirring, 2 minutes. Transfer mixture to small bowl; cool 10 minutes. Refrigerate about 20 minutes or until glaze is spreadable.

prep + cook time 1 hour 10 minutes (+ refrigeration) **serves** 16

chocolate fudge cake

250g dark eating chocolate, chopped
125g butter, chopped
⅔ cup (150g) caster sugar
⅔ cup (100g) self-raising flour
4 eggs, beaten lightly

1 Preheat oven to 180°C/160°C fan-forced. Grease 19cm x 29cm lamington pan; line base and long sides with baking paper, extending paper 5cm above sides.
2 Stir chocolate and butter in medium heatproof bowl over medium saucepan of simmering water (do not allow the water to touch base of bowl); cool.
3 Add remaining ingredients to chocolate mixture; beat on low speed with electric mixer until ingredients are combined. Increase speed to medium; beat about 3 minutes or until mixture is changed in colour and smooth.
4 Pour mixture into pan; bake about 30 minutes. Stand cake in pan 5 minutes; turn, top-side up, onto wire rack to cool. If you like, dust with sifted cocoa powder before cutting into squares.

prep + cook time 50 minutes **serves** 12

chocolate, apricot and hazelnut cake

1⅔ cups (250g) dried apricots,
  chopped finely
½ cup (125ml) water
250g butter, softened
2 cups (440g) firmly packed
  brown sugar
6 eggs
1 cup (150g) plain flour
½ cup (75g) self-raising flour
¼ cup (25g) cocoa powder
1 cup (100g) ground hazelnuts
⅔ cup (160ml) buttermilk

chocolate buttermilk cream
300g milk eating chocolate,
  chopped coarsely
½ cup (125ml) buttermilk
1 cup (160g) icing sugar

1 Bring apricots and the water to the boil in small saucepan. Reduce
heat; simmer, covered, stirring occasionally, about 10 minutes or until
apricots are soft. Cool.
2 Preheat oven to 180°C/160°C fan-forced. Grease deep 22cm-round
cake pan; line with baking paper.
3 Beat butter and sugar in small bowl with electric mixer until light and
fluffy. Beat in eggs, one at a time. Transfer mixture to large bowl; stir in
apricot mixture, sifted flours and cocoa, ground hazelnuts and buttermilk,
in two batches.
4 Spread mixture into pan; bake about 1 hour 50 minutes. Stand cake
in pan 10 minutes; turn, top-side up, onto wire rack to cool.
5 Meanwhile, make chocolate buttermilk cream.
6 Split cold cake into three layers; sandwich layers with two-thirds of the
buttermilk cream. Spread cake with remaining buttermilk cream. Top with
dark chocolate curls, if you like.
chocolate buttermilk cream Stir chocolate and buttermilk in small
heatproof bowl over small saucepan of simmering water until smooth; stir
in sifted icing sugar. Refrigerate, stirring occasionally, about 30 minutes,
or until spreadable.

prep + cook time 2 hours 25 minutes (+ cooling & refrigeration)
serves 12

caramel choc-chip mud cakes

90g white eating chocolate, chopped coarsely
90g unsalted butter, chopped coarsely
½ cup (110g) firmly packed brown sugar
2 tablespoons golden syrup
½ cup (125ml) milk
¾ cup (110g) plain flour
¼ cup (35g) self-raising flour
1 egg
2 tablespoons milk Choc Bits
1 tablespoon icing sugar

1 Preheat oven to 160°C/140°C fan-forced. Grease 9-hole (½-cup/
125ml) friand pan; line bases with baking paper.
2 Stir chocolate, butter, brown sugar, syrup and milk in medium saucepan,
over low heat, until smooth. Cool 15 minutes.
3 Whisk in sifted flours and egg; stir in Choc Bits. Divide mixture among
pan holes.
4 Bake cakes about 25 minutes. Stand cakes in pan 5 minutes; turn,
top-side up, onto wire rack to cool. Serve dusted with sifted icing sugar.

prep + cook time 45 minutes (+ cooling) **makes** 9

marbled chocolate mud cakes

dark mud cake
85g butter, chopped coarsely
75g dark eating chocolate,
　chopped coarsely
⅔ cup (150g) caster sugar
½ cup (125ml) milk
½ cup (75g) plain flour
¼ cup (35g) self-raising flour
1 tablespoon cocoa powder
1 egg
white mud cake
85g butter, chopped coarsely
75g white eating chocolate,
　chopped coarsely

½ cup (110g) caster sugar
⅓ cup (80ml) milk
⅔ cup (100g) plain flour
¼ cup (35g) self-raising flour
1 egg
dark chocolate ganache
⅓ cup (80ml) cream
200g dark eating chocolate,
　chopped coarsely
white chocolate ganache
2 tablespoons cream
100g white eating chocolate,
　chopped coarsely

1 Preheat oven to 160°C/140°C fan-forced. Grease two six-hole (¾-cup/180ml) texas muffin pans.
2 Make dark mud cake by combining butter, chocolate, sugar and milk in medium saucepan; stir over low heat until smooth. Transfer to medium bowl; cool 10 minutes. Whisk in sifted flours and cocoa, then egg.
3 Make white mud cake by combining butter, chocolate, sugar and milk in medium saucepan; stir over low heat until smooth. Transfer to medium bowl; cool 10 minutes. Whisk in sifted flours, then egg.
4 Drop alternate spoonfuls of cake mixtures into pan holes. Pull skewer back and forth through mixture several times for a marbled effect. Bake about 30 minutes.
5 Meanwhile, make dark chocolate and white chocolate ganaches.
6 Stand cakes in pan 5 minute; turn, top-side up, onto wire rack to cool.
7 Spread cakes with dark chocolate ganache; dollop spoonfuls of white chocolate ganache on top. Using palette knife, swirl back and forth through ganache for marbled effect.
dark chocolate ganache Stir cream and chocolate in small saucepan over low heat until smooth. Cool 15 minutes.
white chocolate ganache Stir cream and chocolate in small saucepan over low heat until smooth. Cool 15 minutes.

prep + cook time 1 hour 10 minutes (+ cooling) **makes** 12

choc-cherry cake

370g packet rich chocolate cake mix
1 cup (250ml) vegetable oil
2½ cups (625ml) water
200g dark eating chocolate, melted
1 cup (220g) firmly packed brown sugar
2 eggs
2 cups (300g) plain flour
½ cup (50g) cocoa powder
1 teaspoon bicarbonate of soda
300g frozen cherries, chopped coarsely
chocolate satin icing
200g dark eating chocolate, chopped coarsely
125g butter, chopped coarsely
⅓ cup (80g) sour cream

1 Preheat oven to 180°C/160°C fan-forced. Grease 26.5cm x 36.5cm (4-litre/16-cup) baking dish; line base and long sides with baking paper, extending paper 5cm over sides.
2 Beat cake mix, oil, the water, chocolate, sugar, eggs and sifted dry ingredients in large bowl on low speed with electric mixer until ingredients are combined. Increase speed to medium; beat about 3 minutes or until mixture is smooth and paler in colour. Stir in cherries.
3 Pour mixture into dish; bake about 1 hour 20 minutes. Stand cake in dish 10 minutes; turn, top-side up, onto wire rack to cool.
4 Meanwhile, make chocolate satin icing. Spread cake with icing.
chocolate satin icing Stir chocolate and butter in small saucepan over low heat until smooth; stir in sour cream. Refrigerate 5 minutes or until icing is spreadable.

prep + cook time 1 hour 40 minutes **serves** 30

chocolate sticky date cakes

1¾ cups (250g) seeded dried dates
1⅓ cups (330ml) boiling water
1 teaspoon bicarbonate of soda
125g butter, softened
¾ cup (165g) firmly packed brown sugar
3 eggs
1½ cups (225g) self-raising flour
½ cup (95g) dark Choc Bits
chocolate icing
1½ cups (240g) icing sugar
1 tablespoon cocoa powder
50g butter, melted
2 tablespoons hot water, approximately

1 Preheat oven to 180°C/160°C fan-forced. Grease 16 holes of two 12-hole (⅓-cup/80ml) muffin pans.
2 Bring dates and the water to the boil in small saucepan. Remove from heat; stir in soda, stand 10 minutes. Blend or process mixture until almost smooth. Cool 10 minutes.
3 Beat butter and sugar in small bowl with electric mixer until light and fluffy. Beat in eggs, one at a time. Transfer mixture to large bowl; stir in sifted flour, Choc Bits and date mixture.
4 Spoon mixture into pan holes; bake about 25 minutes. Stand cakes in pan 10 minutes before turning, top-side up, onto wire rack to cool.
5 Meanwhile, make chocolate icing. Spread cakes with icing.
chocolate icing Sift icing sugar and cocoa into small bowl; stir in butter and enough hot water to make icing spreadable.

prep + cook time 45 minutes **makes** 16

chocolate beetroot cake

3 small fresh beetroot (300g), peeled
250g butter, softened
1 cup (220g) firmly packed brown sugar
4 eggs
1⅓ cups (250g) dark Choc Bits
1 cup (150g) plain flour
1 cup (150g) self-raising flour
chocolate ganache
100g dark eating chocolate, chopped coarsely
⅓ cup (80ml) cream

1 Preheat oven to 170°C/150°C fan-forced. Grease 12cm x 22cm loaf pan; line base and long sides with baking paper, extending paper 5cm over sides.
2 Grate beetroot coarsely.
3 Beat butter and sugar in small bowl with electric mixer until light and fluffy. Beat in eggs, one at a time (mixture might curdle at this stage, but will come together later). Transfer mixture to large bowl; stir in Choc Bits and sifted flours in two batches, then beetroot.
4 Spread mixture into pan; bake about 1½ hours. Stand cake in pan 5 minutes; turn, top-side up, onto wire rack to cool.
5 Meanwhile, make chocolate ganache. Spread cake with ganache.
chocolate ganache Stir ingredients in small saucepan over low heat until smooth; transfer to small bowl. Cover; refrigerate about 40 minutes or until ganache is spreadable. Beat ganache with electric mixer until fluffy and paler in colour.

prep + cook time 2 hours (+ refrigeration) **serves** 12

gluten-free chocolate hazelnut cake

This recipe is gluten-free, yeast-free and wheat-free.

100g dairy-free spread
½ cup (110g) firmly packed brown sugar
2 eggs
¼ cup (60ml) milk
¾ cup (75g) ground hazelnuts
¾ cup (100g) gluten-free self-raising flour
2 tablespoons cocoa powder
fudge frosting
¼ cup (55g) caster sugar
50g dairy-free spread
2 tablespoons water
¾ cup (120g) pure icing sugar
2 tablespoons cocoa powder

1 Preheat oven to 180°C/160°C fan-forced. Grease shallow 22cm-square cake pan; line base and sides with baking paper, extending paper 5cm over edges.
2 Beat spread and sugar in medium bowl with electric mixer until changed to a paler colour. Beat in eggs, one at a time. Stir in milk, ground hazelnuts, sifted flour and cocoa, in two batches.
3 Spread mixture into pan; bake about 20 minutes. Stand cake in pan 10 minutes; turn, top-side up, onto wire rack to cool.
4 Meanwhile, make fudge frosting. Spread cold cake with frosting.
fudge frosting Stir caster sugar, spread and the water in small saucepan over low heat until sugar dissolves. Transfer to medium bowl; gradually stir in sifted icing sugar and cocoa until smooth. Cover; refrigerate 20 minutes. Beat frosting with electric mixer until spreadable.

prep + cook time 40 minutes (+ refrigeration) **serves** 25

mississippi mud cake

250g butter, chopped coarsely
150g dark eating chocolate, chopped coarsely
2 cups (440g) caster sugar
1 cup (250ml) hot water
⅓ cup (80ml) coffee-flavoured liqueur
1 tablespoon instant coffee granules
1½ cups (225g) plain flour
¼ cup (35g) self-raising flour
¼ cup (25g) cocoa powder
2 eggs, beaten lightly

1 Preheat oven to 160°C/140°C fan-forced. Grease deep 20cm-round cake pan; line base and side with baking paper.
2 Place butter, chocolate, sugar, the water, liqueur and coffee powder in medium saucepan. Using wooden spoon, stir mixture over low heat until chocolate melts. Transfer mixture to large bowl; cool 15 minutes.
3 Whisk combined sifted flours and cocoa into chocolate mixture, then whisk in eggs. Pour mixture into pan.
4 Bake cake about 1½ hours. (Cover cake loosely with foil during baking if it starts to overbrown.) Stand cake in pan 30 minutes; turn, top-side up, onto wire rack to cool. Dust with sifted cocoa, if you like.

prep + cook time 2 hours 10 minutes (+ cooling & standing)
serves 16

SPONGE CAKES

grated chocolate roll

4 eggs, separated
½ cup (110g) caster sugar
2 tablespoons hot water
60g dark eating chocolate, grated
½ cup (75g) self-raising flour
2 tablespoons caster sugar, extra
vanilla cream
¾ cup (180ml) thickened cream
2 teaspoons icing sugar
1 teaspoon vanilla extract

1 Preheat oven to 180°C/160°C fan-forced. Grease a 26cm x 32cm swiss roll pan; line base with baking paper, extending paper 5cm over long sides.
2 Beat egg yolks and sugar in small bowl with electric mixer about 5 minutes or until thick and creamy. Transfer mixture to large bowl; fold in hot water and chocolate, then fold in sifted flour.
3 Beat egg whites in small bowl with electric mixer until soft peaks form; fold into chocolate mixture.
4 Pour mixture into pan; bake about 12 minutes.
5 Meanwhile, place a piece of baking paper cut the same size as pan on bench; sprinkle with extra sugar. Turn hot sponge onto paper; peel away lining paper. Using paper as a guide, loosely roll sponge from long side. Stand 2 minutes; unroll. Cool; trim all sides of sponge.
6 Make vanilla cream.
7 Spread sponge with vanilla cream. Using paper as a guide, roll sponge from long side.
vanilla cream Beat ingredients in small bowl with electric mixer until soft peaks form.

prep + cook time 30 minutes (+ refrigeration) **serves** 10

ginger sponge

5 eggs, separated
¾ cup (165g) caster sugar
1 tablespoon golden syrup
⅓ cup (50g) self-raising flour
⅓ cup (50g) cornflour
3 teaspoons ground ginger
1 teaspoon ground cinnamon
2 teaspoons cocoa powder
¾ cup (180ml) thickened cream, whipped

1 Preheat oven to 180°C/160°C fan-forced. Grease and flour two deep 20cm-round cake pans; line bases with baking paper.
2 Beat egg whites in medium bowl with electric mixer until soft peaks form; gradually add sugar, beating until sugar is dissolved between additions. Beat in egg yolks and golden syrup. Fold in triple-sifted dry ingredients.
3 Divide mixture between pans; bake about 18 minutes. Immediately turn sponges, top-side up, onto baking-paper-covered wire rack to cool.
4 Sandwich cakes with whipped cream. Serve dusted with a little sifted icing sugar, if you like.

prep + cook time 40 minutes **serves** 10

wheat-free sponge

3 eggs
½ cup (110g) caster sugar
¾ cup (110g) 100% maize cornflour

1 Preheat oven to 180°C/160°C fan-forced. Grease 20cm-round cake pan; line base with baking paper.
2 Beat eggs in small bowl with electric mixer about 10 minutes or until thick and creamy. Gradually add sugar, beating until dissolved between additions. Fold in triple-sifted flour.
3 Spread mixture into pan; bake about 20 minutes. Turn sponge onto a wire rack to cool. Dust with a little sifted pure icing sugar, if you like.

prep + cook time 35 minutes **serves** 8

pineapple jelly cakes

6 eggs
⅔ cup (150g) caster sugar
⅓ cup (50g) cornflour
½ cup (75g) plain flour
⅓ cup (50g) self-raising flour
80g packet pineapple jelly crystals
1 cup (80g) desiccated coconut
1 cup (75g) shredded coconut
⅔ cup (160ml) thickened cream, whipped

1 Preheat oven to 180°C/160°C fan-forced. Grease 19cm x 30cm lamington pan; line base and long sides with baking paper, extending paper 5cm over sides.
2 Beat eggs in medium bowl with electric mixer about 10 minutes or until thick and creamy. Gradually add sugar, beating until dissolved between each addition. Fold in triple-sifted flours.
3 Spread mixture into pan; bake about 30 minutes. Turn cake onto baking-paper-covered wire rack to cool.
4 Meanwhile, make jelly as per packet instructions; refrigerate until set to the consistency of unbeaten egg white.
5 Trim all sides of cake. Cut cake into 20 squares; dip each square in jelly, drain off excess. Toss squares in combined coconuts. Place on tray; refrigerate 30 minutes.
6 Halve cakes horizontally; sandwich cakes with whipped cream.

prep + cook time 1 hour (+ refrigeration) **makes** 20

featherlight sponge cake

4 eggs
¾ cup (165g) caster sugar
⅔ cup (100g) wheaten cornflour
¼ cup (30g) custard powder
1 teaspoon cream of tartar
½ teaspoon bicarbonate of soda
⅓ cup (110g) apricot jam
300ml thickened cream, whipped

1 Preheat oven to 180°C/160°C fan-forced. Grease and flour two deep 22cm-round cake pans; shake away excess flour.
2 Beat eggs and sugar in small bowl with electric mixer until mixture is thick and creamy and sugar is dissolved. Transfer mixture to large bowl; fold in triple-sifted dry ingredients.
3 Divide mixture between pans; bake about 20 minutes. Turn sponges, top-side up, onto baking-paper-covered wire rack to cool.
4 Sandwich sponges with jam and cream.

prep + cook time 40 minutes **serves** 10

passionfruit curd sponge cakes

You need about 4 passionfruit to get the required amount of pulp.

3 eggs
½ cup (110g) caster sugar
¾ cup (110g) self-raising flour
20g butter
¼ cup (60ml) boiling water
passionfruit curd
⅓ cup (80ml) passionfruit pulp
½ cup (110g) caster sugar
2 eggs, beaten lightly
125g unsalted butter, chopped coarsely

1 Make passionfruit curd.
2 Preheat oven to 180°C/160°C fan-forced. Grease 12-hole (½-cup/ 125ml) oval friand pan with softened butter; dust lightly with flour.
3 Beat eggs in small bowl with electric mixer until thick and creamy. Gradually add sugar, beating until dissolved between additions. Transfer mixture to large bowl. Fold in sifted flour then combined butter and the boiling water.
4 Spoon mixture into pan holes; bake about 12 minutes. Working quickly, loosen edges of cakes from pan using a small knife; turn immediately onto baking-paper-covered wire racks to cool.
5 Split cooled cakes in half. Spread cut-sides with curd; replace tops. Serve lightly dusted with a little sifted icing sugar.
passionfruit curd Stir ingredients in medium heatproof bowl over medium saucepan of simmering water about 10 minutes or until mixture coats the back of a wooden spoon. Cover; refrigerate 3 hours.

prep + cook time 40 minutes (+ refrigeration & cooling) **makes** 12

sponge roll with jam and cream

3 eggs
⅔ cup (150g) caster sugar
½ cup (75g) wheaten cornflour
2 tablespoons custard powder
¾ teaspoon cream of tartar
½ teaspoon bicarbonate of soda
⅓ cup (110g) raspberry jam
¾ cup (180ml) thickened cream, whipped

1 Preheat oven to 180°C/160°C fan-forced. Grease 25cm x 30cm swiss roll pan; line base and long sides with baking paper, extending paper 5cm over sides.
2 Beat eggs and ½ cup of the caster sugar in small bowl with electric mixer until thick and creamy and sugar is dissolved. Fold in triple-sifted dry ingredients.
3 Spread mixture into pan; bake about 12 minutes.
4 Meanwhile, place piece of baking paper cut the same size as pan on bench; sprinkle with remaining caster sugar. Turn sponge onto paper; peel lining paper away. Cool; trim all sides of sponge.
5 Spread sponge with jam then cream. Using paper as a guide, roll sponge from short side. Cover with plastic wrap; refrigerate 30 minutes.

prep + cook time 40 minutes (+ refrigeration) **serves** 10

spiced sponge with pistachio honey cream

4 eggs
¾ cup (165g) firmly packed dark brown sugar
1 cup (150g) wheaten cornflour
1 teaspoon cream of tartar
½ teaspoon bicarbonate of soda
1 teaspoon mixed spice
½ teaspoon ground cardamom
pistachio honey cream
300ml thickened cream
1 tablespoon honey
¼ cup (30g) finely chopped roasted unsalted pistachios

1 Preheat oven to 180°C/160°C fan-forced. Grease two deep 23cm-round cake pans.
2 Beat eggs and sugar in small bowl with electric mixer about 10 minutes or until sugar dissolves and mixture is thick and creamy. Transfer mixture to large bowl; gently fold in triple-sifted dry ingredients.
3 Divide mixture between pans; bake about 18 minutes. Turn sponges, top-side up, onto baking-paper-covered wire rack to cool.
4 Meanwhile, make pistachio honey cream. Sandwich sponges with cream; dust with a little sifted icing sugar.
pistachio honey cream Beat cream and honey in small bowl with electric mixer until soft peaks form; fold in nuts.

prep + cook time 40 minutes **serves** 10

ginger powder puffs

2 eggs
⅓ cup (75g) caster sugar
2 tablespoons cornflour
1 tablespoon plain flour
2 tablespoons self-raising flour
1 teaspoon cocoa powder
1½ teaspoons ground ginger
¼ teaspoon ground cinnamon
orange cream
⅔ cup (160ml) thickened cream
2 tablespoons icing sugar
1 teaspoon finely grated orange rind

1 Preheat oven to 180°C/160°C fan-forced. Grease and flour two 12-hole (1½-tablespoon/30ml) shallow round-based patty pans.
2 Beat eggs and sugar in small bowl with electric mixer until thick and creamy. Fold in triple-sifted dry ingredients. Divide mixture among pan holes. Bake about 8 minutes.
3 Working quickly, loosen edges of cakes using palette knife, then turn immediately onto baking-paper-lined wire racks to cool.
4 Meanwhile, make orange cream.
5 Just before serving, sandwich puffs together with orange cream. Serve lightly dusted with a little sifted icing sugar.
orange cream Beat cream and sifted icing sugar in small bowl with electric mixer until firm peaks form; fold in rind.

prep + cook time 30 minutes **makes** 12

genoise sponge

4 eggs
½ cup (110g) caster sugar
⅔ cup (100g) plain flour
60g butter, melted
300ml thickened cream
1 tablespoon icing sugar
¼ cup (80g) strawberry jam, warmed
500g strawberries, sliced thinly
1 tablespoon icing sugar, extra

1 Preheat oven to 180°C/160°C fan-forced. Grease deep 20cm-round cake pan; line base with baking paper.
2 Combine eggs and sugar in large heatproof bowl, place over saucepan of simmering water (do not allow water to touch base of bowl); beat with electric mixer about 10 minutes or until mixture is thick and creamy. Remove bowl from saucepan; beat mixture until it returns to room temperature.
3 Sift half the flour over egg mixture; carefully fold in flour. Sift remaining flour into bowl; fold into mixture. Working quickly, fold in melted butter.
4 Pour mixture into pan; bake about 20 minutes. Turn immediately, top-side up, onto baking-paper-covered wire rack to cool.
5 Beat cream and sifted icing sugar in small bowl with electric mixer until soft peaks form. Split sponge in half; place one half, cut-side up, on serving plate. Spread with jam and cream; top with strawberries, then remaining sponge. Decorate cake with extra sifted icing sugar and strawberries, if you like.

prep + cook time 1 hour (+ cooling) **serves** 8

honey sponge cake

2 eggs
½ cup (110g) caster sugar
⅓ cup (50g) wheaten cornflour
1½ tablespoons custard powder
1 teaspoon mixed spice
½ teaspoon cream of tartar
¼ teaspoon bicarbonate of soda
300ml thickened cream
2 tablespoons honey
1 tablespoon icing sugar

1 Preheat oven to 180°C/160°C fan-forced. Grease 25cm x 30cm swiss roll pan; line base and long sides with baking paper, extending paper 5cm over sides.
2 Beat eggs and ⅓ cup of the caster sugar in small bowl with electric mixer about 10 minutes or until thick and creamy. Fold triple-sifted dry ingredients into egg mixture.
3 Spread mixture into pan; bake 10 minutes.
4 Meanwhile, place piece of baking paper cut the same size as pan on bench; sprinkle with remaining caster sugar. Turn hot sponge onto paper; peel away lining paper. Cool; trim all sides of sponge.
5 Beat cream and honey in small bowl with electric mixer until firm peaks form.
6 Cut sponge widthways into three equal-sized rectangles. Place one piece of sponge on serving plate; spread with half the cream mixture. Top with second piece of sponge and remaining cream. Finish with remaining sponge piece then dust with sifted icing sugar.

prep + cook time 30 minutes **serves** 6

victoria sponge sandwich

250g butter
1 teaspoon vanilla extract
1 cup (220g) caster sugar
4 eggs
⅓ cup (80ml) milk
2 cups (300g) self-raising flour
⅓ cup (110g) raspberry jam, warmed

1 Preheat oven to 180°C/160°C fan-forced. Grease two deep 20cm-round cake pans; line bases with baking paper.
2 Beat butter, extract and sugar in small bowl with electric mixer until light and fluffy. Beat in eggs, one at a time. Add milk and beat well. Transfer mixture to large bowl. Stir in half the sifted flour, then remaining sifted flour; stir until the mixture is smooth.
3 Divide mixture between pans; bake about 30 minutes.
4 Turn cakes onto baking-paper-covered wire rack to cool. Sandwich cakes with jam; dust with a little sifted icing sugar.

prep + cook time 50 minutes **serves** 10

chocolate sponge

3 eggs
½ cup (110g) caster sugar
¼ cup (35g) cornflour
¼ cup (35g) plain flour
¼ cup (35g) self-raising flour
2 tablespoons cocoa powder
300ml thickened cream, whipped
coffee icing
3 teaspoons instant coffee granules
2 tablespoons milk
1½ cups (240g) icing sugar
1 teaspoon soft butter

1 Preheat oven to 180°C/160°C fan-forced. Grease deep 22cm-round cake pan; line base with baking paper.
2 Beat eggs in small bowl with electric mixer until thick and creamy. Gradually add sugar, beating until dissolved between each addition. Transfer mixture to large bowl; gently fold in triple-sifted dry ingredients.
3 Spread mixture into pan; bake 25 minutes. Turn sponge, top-side up, onto baking-paper-covered wire rack to cool.
4 Make coffee icing.
5 Split sponge in half; sandwich with cream. Spread top with icing; leave to set before cutting.
coffee icing Stir coffee and milk in small bowl until dissolved. Sift icing sugar into small bowl; stir in butter and enough of the coffee mixture to give a firm paste. Place bowl over small saucepan of simmering water; stir until icing is spreadable (do not overheat). Use immediately.

prep + cook time 40 minutes (+ cooling) **serves** 10

lamingtons

6 eggs
⅔ cup (150g) caster sugar
⅓ cup (50g) cornflour
½ cup (75g) plain flour
⅓ cup (50g) self-raising flour
2 cups (160g) desiccated coconut
icing
4 cups (640g) icing sugar
½ cup (50g) cocoa powder
15g butter, melted
1 cup (250ml) milk

1 Preheat oven to 180°C/160°C fan-forced. Grease 20cm x 30cm lamington pan; line with baking paper, extending paper 5cm over long sides.
2 Beat eggs in medium bowl with electric mixer about 10 minutes or until thick and creamy. Gradually add sugar, beating until dissolved between each addition. Fold in triple-sifted flours.
3 Spread mixture into pan; bake about 35 minutes. Turn cake onto baking-paper-covered wire rack to cool.
4 Meanwhile, make icing.
5 Cut cake into 16 pieces; dip each square in icing, drain off excess. Toss squares in coconut. Place lamingtons onto wire rack to set.
icing Sift icing sugar and cocoa into medium heatproof bowl; stir in butter and milk. Place bowl over medium saucepan of simmering water; stir until icing is of a coating consistency.

prep + cook time 55 minutes (+ cooling) **makes** 16

white chocolate lamingtons

6 eggs
⅔ cup (150g) caster sugar
80g white eating chocolate, chopped finely
½ cup (75g) plain flour
⅓ cup (50g) self-raising flour
⅓ cup (50g) cornflour
2 cups (150g) shredded coconut
100g white eating chocolate, grated finely
icing
4 cups (640g) icing sugar
¾ cup (180ml) milk

1 Preheat oven to 180°C/160°C fan-forced. Grease 23cm-square slab cake pan; line base and sides with baking paper, extending paper 5cm over sides.
2 Beat eggs in medium bowl with electric mixer about 10 minutes or until thick and creamy. Gradually add caster sugar, beating until dissolved between each addition. Fold in chopped chocolate and triple-sifted flours.
3 Spread mixture into pan; bake about 35 minutes. Turn cake onto baking-paper-covered wire rack to cool; refrigerate until required.
4 Make icing.
5 Cut cold cake into 25 squares; dip each square in icing, drain off excess. Toss squares in combined coconut and grated chocolate. Place lamingtons onto wire rack to set.
icing Sift icing sugar into medium heatproof bowl; stir in milk. Place bowl over medium saucepan of simmering water; stir until icing is of a coating consistency

prep + cook time 1 hour 10 minutes (+ cooling) **makes** 25

strawberry jelly cakes

6 eggs
⅔ cup (150g) caster sugar
⅓ cup (50g) cornflour
½ cup (75g) plain flour
⅓ cup (50g) self-raising flour
80g packet strawberry jelly crystals
2 cups (160g) desiccated coconut
300ml thickened cream, whipped

1 Preheat oven to 180°C/160°C fan-forced. Grease 20cm x 30cm lamington pan; line base and long sides with baking paper, extending paper 5cm over sides.
2 Beat eggs in medium bowl with electric mixer about 10 minutes or until thick and creamy. Gradually add sugar, beating until dissolved between each addition. Fold in triple-sifted flours.
3 Spread mixture into pan; bake about 35 minutes. Turn cake onto baking-paper-covered wire rack to cool.
4 Meanwhile, make jelly as per packet instructions; refrigerate until set to the consistency of unbeaten egg white.
5 Trim all sides of cake. Cut cake into 15 squares; dip each square in jelly, drain off excess. Toss squares in coconut. Place on tray; refrigerate 30 minutes.
6 Halve cakes horizontally; sandwich cakes with whipped cream.

prep + cook time 50 minutes (+ refrigeration) **makes** 15

rhubarb and pear sponge

825g can pear slices in natural juice
800g rhubarb, trimmed, cut into 4cm pieces
2 tablespoons caster sugar
2 eggs
⅓ cup (75g) caster sugar, extra
2 tablespoons plain flour
2 tablespoons self-raising flour
2 tablespoons cornflour

1 Preheat oven to 180°C/160°C fan-forced.
2 Drain pears; reserve ¾ cup (180ml) of the juice.
3 Place reserved juice, rhubarb and sugar in large saucepan; cook,
stirring occasionally, about 5 minutes or until rhubarb is just tender.
Stir in pears. Pour mixture into deep 1.75-litre (7-cup) ovenproof dish.
4 Meanwhile, beat eggs in small bowl with electric mixer until thick and
creamy. Gradually add extra sugar, 1 tablespoon at a time, beating until
sugar dissolves between additions. Gently fold in combined sifted flours.
5 Spread sponge mixture over hot rhubarb mixture; bake 45 minutes or
until browned lightly and cooked through. Serve dusted with a little sifted
icing sugar.

prep + cook time 1 hour 10 minutes **serves** 6

ginger cream roll

3 eggs
⅔ cup (150g) caster sugar
⅔ cup (100g) wheaten cornflour
1 teaspoon cream of tartar
½ teaspoon bicarbonate of soda
1 teaspoon cocoa powder
2 teaspoons ground ginger
½ teaspoon ground cinnamon
ginger cream filling
¾ cup (180ml) thickened cream
2 tablespoons golden syrup
1 teaspoon ground ginger

1 Preheat oven to 180°C/160°C fan-forced. Grease 25cm x 30cm swiss roll pan; line base with baking paper, extending paper 5cm over long sides.
2 Beat eggs and ½ cup of the sugar in small bowl with electric mixer until thick and creamy and sugar is dissolved. Fold in triple-sifted dry ingredients.
3 Spread mixture into pan; bake about 12 minutes.
4 Meanwhile, place a piece of baking paper cut the same size as pan on bench; sprinkle with remaining sugar. Turn hot sponge onto paper; peel away lining paper. Cool; trim all sides of sponge.
5 Make ginger cream filling.
6 Spread sponge with filling. Using paper as a guide, roll sponge from long side. Cover with plastic wrap; refrigerate 30 minutes.
ginger cream filling Beat ingredients in small bowl with electric mixer until firm peaks form.

prep + cook time 40 minutes (+ refrigeration) **serves** 10

FRUIT CAKES

boiled fruit cake

1kg (5 cups) mixed dried fruit, chopped coarsely
250g butter, chopped coarsely
1 ¼ cups (275g) firmly packed brown sugar
1 cup (250ml) sherry
¼ cup (60ml) water
2 teaspoons finely grated orange rind
4 eggs, beaten lightly
1 ½ cups (225g) plain flour
½ cup (75g) self-raising flour
2 teaspoons mixed spice
½ cup (60g) pecans
¾ cup (105g) macadamias

1 Line deep 22cm-round cake pan with three thicknesses of baking paper, extending paper 5cm above side.
2 Stir fruit, butter, sugar, ¾ cup of the sherry and the water in large saucepan over medium heat until butter is melted and sugar dissolved. Bring to the boil. Remove from heat; transfer to large bowl, cool.
3 Preheat oven to 150°C/130°C fan-forced.
4 Stir rind and eggs into fruit mixture then sifted dry ingredients. Spread mixture into pan; top with nuts.
5 Bake cake about 3 hours. Brush hot cake with remaining sherry; cover with foil, cool in pan overnight.

prep + cook time 3 hours 30 minutes (+ cooling) **serves** 20
tip This is a rich cake and will keep well. Store it in the fridge in an airtight container.

hummingbird cakes with coconut crust

You need about 2 large overripe bananas (460g) to get the required amount of mashed banana.

440g can crushed pineapple in syrup
1 cup (150g) plain flour
½ cup (75g) self-raising flour
½ teaspoon bicarbonate of soda
½ teaspoon ground cinnamon
½ teaspoon ground ginger
1 cup (220g) firmly packed brown sugar
½ cup (40g) desiccated coconut
1 cup mashed banana
2 eggs, beaten lightly
¾ cup (180ml) vegetable oil
coconut crust
3 cups (225g) shredded coconut
½ cup (110g) firmly packed brown sugar
3 eggs, beaten lightly

1 Preheat oven to 180°C/160°C fan-forced. Line three six-hole
(⅓-cup/80ml) muffin pans with paper cases.
2 Drain pineapple over medium bowl, pressing with spoon to extract
as much syrup as possible. Reserve ¼ cup of the syrup.
3 Sift flours, soda, spices and sugar into large bowl. Stir in drained
pineapple, reserved syrup, coconut, banana, egg and oil.
4 Spoon mixture into paper cases; bake 10 minutes.
5 Meanwhile, make coconut crust.
6 Spoon crust over cakes; return to oven, bake about 15 minutes.
Stand cakes in pans 5 minutes; turn, top-side up, onto wire rack to cool.
Serve lightly dusted with sifted icing sugar, if you like.
coconut crust Combine ingredients in medium bowl.

prep + cook time 50 minutes **makes** 18

walnut and prune loaf

100g butter, softened
¾ cup (165g) caster sugar
2 eggs
2 cups (320g) wholemeal self-raising flour
1 cup (280g) yogurt
⅓ cup (80ml) orange juice
1 cup (190g) finely chopped seeded prunes
⅔ cup (80g) finely chopped roasted walnuts

1 Preheat oven to 180°C/160°C fan-forced. Grease 12cm x 22cm loaf pan; line base and long sides with baking paper, extending paper 5cm over sides.
2 Beat butter, sugar, eggs, sifted flour, yogurt and juice in medium bowl on low speed with electric mixer until combined. Stir in prunes and nuts.
3 Spread mixture into pan; bake about 1¼ hours. Stand loaf in pan 10 minutes; turn, top-side up, onto wire rack to cool.

prep + cook time 1 hour 45 minutes **serves** 10

tropical fruit cakes

8 slices glacé pineapple (345g)
1 cup (180g) dried papaya
½ cup (90g) dried mango
½ cup (115g) glacé ginger
1 cup (140g) macadamias
1 cup (170g) brazil nuts
2 eggs
½ cup (110g) firmly packed
  brown sugar
1 tablespoon coconut-flavoured
  liqueur
100g butter, melted
⅓ cup (50g) plain four
¼ cup (35g) self-raising flour
¼ cup (80g) apricot jam,
  warmed, sieved

fruit and nut topping
3 slices glacé pineapple (170g)
¾ cup (135g) dried papaya
¼ cup (55g) glacé ginger
⅓ cup (45g) macadamias
⅓ cup (55g) brazil nuts
½ cup (25g) coarsely grated
  fresh coconut

1 Preheat oven to 150°C/130°C fan-forced. Grease six deep 8cm-round cake pans; line with baking paper.
2 Coarsely chop fruit. Combine fruit and nuts in large bowl.
3 Beat eggs and sugar in small bowl with electric mixer until thick and creamy. Add liqueur, butter and sifted flours; beat until combined. Stir egg mixture into fruit mixture. Press mixture firmly into pans.
4 Make fruit and nut topping.
5 Gently press topping evenly over cake mixture; bake about 1¾ hours.
6 Turn cakes, top-side up, onto wire rack; brush tops with jam. Cool.
fruit and nut topping Coarsely chop fruit; combine with nuts and coconut in medium bowl.

prep + cook time 2 hours 15 minutes (+ cooling) **makes** 6

apple streusel cake

200g butter, softened
2 teaspoons finely grated
  lemon rind
⅔ cup (150g) caster sugar
3 eggs
1 cup (150g) self-raising flour
½ cup (75g) plain flour
⅓ cup (80ml) milk
5 medium apples (750g)
25g butter, extra
⅓ cup (75g) firmly packed
  brown sugar

streusel
½ cup (75g) plain flour
¼ cup (35g) self-raising flour
⅓ cup (75g) firmly packed
  brown sugar
½ teaspoon ground cinnamon
80g butter, chopped finely

1 Preheat oven to 180°C/160°C fan-forced. Grease deep 23cm-round cake pan; line with baking paper.

2 Make streusel.

3 Beat butter, rind and caster sugar in small bowl with electric mixer until light and fluffy. Beat in eggs, one at a time. Transfer to large bowl; stir in sifted flours and milk, in two batches.

4 Spread mixture into pan; bake 25 minutes.

5 Meanwhile, peel, core and quarter apples; slice thinly. Melt extra butter in large frying pan; cook apple, stirring, about 5 minutes or until browned lightly. Add brown sugar; cook, stirring, about 5 minutes or until mixture thickens slightly. Set aside.

6 Remove cake from oven. Working quickly, top cake with apple mixture; coarsely grate streusel over apple. Return to oven; bake about 25 minutes. Stand cake in pan 10 minutes; turn, top-side up, onto wire rack to cool. Serve cake warm or cold.

streusel Process flours, sugar and cinnamon until combined. Add butter; process until ingredients just come together. Wrap in plastic wrap; freeze about 1 hour or until firm.

prep + cook time 1 hour 15 minutes (+ freezing) **serves** 16

banana cake with passionfruit icing

You need about 2 large overripe bananas (460g) to get the required
amount of mashed banana, as well 2 large passionfruit.

125g butter, softened
¾ cup (165g) firmly packed brown sugar
2 eggs
1½ cups (225g) self-raising flour
½ teaspoon bicarbonate of soda
1 teaspoon mixed spice
1 cup mashed banana
½ cup (120g) sour cream
¼ cup (60ml) milk
passionfruit icing
1½ cups (240g) icing sugar
1 teaspoon soft butter
2 tablespoons passionfruit pulp, approximately

1 Preheat oven to 180°C/160°C. Grease 15cm x 25cm loaf pan;
line base with baking paper.
2 Beat butter and sugar in small bowl with electric mixer until light
and fluffy. Beat in eggs, one at a time. Transfer to large bowl; stir in
sifted dry ingredients, banana, sour cream and milk.
3 Spread mixture into pan; bake about 50 minutes. Stand cake in pan
5 minutes; turn, top-side up, onto wire rack to cool.
4 Meanwhile, make passionfruit icing. Spread cake with icing.
passionfruit icing Combine ingredients in medium bowl.

prep + cook time 1 hour 25 minutes (+ cooling) **serves** 10

banana loaves with muesli topping

You need about 1 large overripe banana (230g) to get the required amount of mashed banana.

75g butter, softened
⅓ cup (75g) firmly packed brown sugar
1 egg
¾ cup (110g) self-raising flour
¼ teaspoon bicarbonate of soda
½ cup mashed overripe banana
¼ cup (60g) sour cream
1 tablespoon milk
¾ cup (75g) untoasted muesli
¼ cup (35g) dried cranberries

1 Preheat oven to 180°C/160°C fan-forced. Grease six holes of 8-hole (¾-cup/180ml) petite loaf pan.
2 Beat butter and sugar in small bowl with electric mixer until light and fluffy. Beat in egg. Stir in sifted dry ingredients, banana, sour cream and milk.
3 Spoon mixture into greased pan holes; sprinkle with combined muesli and cranberries.
4 Bake loaves about 25 minutes. Stand loaves in pan 5 minutes; turn, top-side up, onto wire rack to cool.

prep + cook time 45 minutes **makes** 6

mini choc-chip banana loaves

You need about 2 large overripe bananas (460g) to get the required amount of mashed banana.

1 cup mashed overripe banana
¾ cup (165g) firmly packed brown sugar
2 eggs
60g butter, melted
¼ cup (60ml) buttermilk
⅔ cup (100g) self-raising flour
⅔ cup (100g) wholemeal self-raising flour
½ cup (95g) milk Choc Bits

1 Preheat oven to 180°C/160°C fan-forced. Grease 8-hole (¾-cup/180ml) mini loaf pan; line base and two short sides with baking paper.
2 Combine banana and sugar in large bowl; stir in eggs, butter and buttermilk, then sifted flours and Choc Bits.
3 Spoon mixture into pan holes; bake about 20 minutes. Stand loaves in pan 5 minutes; turn, top-side up, onto wire rack to cool. Serve warm with butter, if you like.

prep + cook time 40 minutes **makes** 8

white christmas cake

½ cup (115g) coarsely chopped
   glacé pineapple
¾ cup (150g) halved red and
   green glacé cherries
½ cup (115g) coarsely chopped
   glacé ginger
¼ cup (60g) coarsely chopped
   glacé figs
¼ cup (60g) coarsely chopped
   glacé apricots
⅓ cup (55g) mixed peel
1 cup (110g) coarsely chopped
   walnuts
1 tablespoon marmalade

2 teaspoons finely grated
   lemon rind
1 tablespoon honey
¼ cup (60ml) sweet sherry
1 teaspoon vanilla extract
250g butter, softened
1 cup (220g) caster sugar
4 eggs
2¼ cups (335g) plain flour
fluffy frosting
1 cup (220g) caster sugar
⅓ cup (80ml) water
2 egg whites

1 Combine fruits, nuts, marmalade, rind, honey, sherry and extract in
large bowl; cover, stand overnight.
2 Line deep 20cm-square or deep 22cm-round cake pan with two layers
baking paper, bringing paper 5cm above side(s) of pan.
3 Preheat oven to 150°C/130°C fan-forced.
4 Beat butter until smooth; add sugar, beat until combined. Beat in eggs,
one at a time. Mix egg mixture into fruit mixture; stir in sifted flour.
5 Spread mixture into pan; bake about 2½ hours. Cover cake with foil;
cool in pan overnight.
6 Make fluffy frosting. Spread cake all over with frosting. Decorate with
Christmas ornaments before frosting sets.
fluffy frosting Stir sugar and the water in small saucepan over heat,
without boiling, until sugar is dissolved. Boil, uncovered, without stirring,
about 5 minutes or until syrup reaches 116°C on a candy thermometer.
Syrup should be thick but not coloured. Remove from heat, allow bubbles
to subside. Beat egg whites in small bowl with electric mixer until soft
peaks form. While motor is operating, add hot syrup in a thin steady
stream; beat on high speed about 10 minutes or until mixture is thick.

prep + cook time 3 hours (+ standing & cooling) **serves** 20

moist whole orange cake

2 medium oranges (480g)
⅔ cup (110g) blanched almonds, roasted
1 cup (220g) caster sugar
1 teaspoon baking powder
6 eggs
2 cups (240g) ground almonds
2 tablespoons plain flour

1 Place unpeeled oranges in medium saucepan; cover with cold water, bring to the boil. Boil, covered, 30 minutes; drain. Repeat process with fresh water, boil about 1 hour or until oranges are tender; cool.
2 Preheat oven to 180°C/160°C fan-forced. Grease deep 22cm-round cake pan; line base and side with baking paper.
3 Process blanched almonds with 2 tablespoons of the sugar until finely chopped.
4 Trim ends off oranges and discard. Halve oranges; remove and discard seeds. Process oranges, including rind, with baking powder until mixture is pulpy.
5 Beat eggs and remaining sugar in medium bowl with electric mixer about 3 minutes or until fluffy and pale in colour. Fold in almond mixture, ground almonds, flour and orange pulp.
6 Pour mixture into pan; bake about 1 hour. Cool in pan.
7 Turn cake onto serving plate and dust with sifted icing sugar, if you like.

prep + cook time 3 hours 10 minutes (+ cooling) **serves** 10

lumberjack cake

2 large apples (400g), peeled,
  cored, chopped finely
1 cup (150g) finely chopped
  seeded dried dates
1 teaspoon bicarbonate of soda
1 cup (250ml) boiling water
125g butter, softened
1 teaspoon vanilla extract
1 cup (220g) caster sugar
1 egg
1½ cups (225g) plain flour

coconut topping
60g butter, chopped
½ cup (110g) firmly packed
  brown sugar
½ cup (125ml) milk
⅔ cup (50g) shredded coconut

1 Preheat oven to 180°C/160°C fan-forced. Grease deep 23cm-square
cake pan; line base and sides with baking paper.
2 Combine apple, dates and soda in large bowl, stir in the water; cover
bowl with plastic wrap, stand 10 minutes.
3 Meanwhile, beat butter, extract, sugar and egg in small bowl with
electric mixer until light and fluffy. Add butter mixture to apple mixture;
stir to combine. Add sifted flour; stir to combine.
4 Pour mixture into pan; bake about 50 minutes.
5 Meanwhile, make coconut topping.
6 Remove cake carefully from oven to bench. Using metal spatula,
carefully spread warm topping evenly over cake; return to oven,
bake about 20 minutes or until topping is browned. Stand cake in
pan 5 minutes; turn, top-side up, onto wire rack to cool.
coconut topping Stir ingredients in medium saucepan over low heat
until butter melts and sugar dissolves.

prep + cook time 1 hour 40 minutes **serves** 12

mini sultana loaves

125g butter, melted
2⅓ cups (375g) sultanas
⅔ cup (150g) caster sugar
2 eggs
⅓ cup (80ml) buttermilk
½ cup (75g) plain flour
¾ cup (110g) self-raising flour
lemon glacé Icing
1½ cups (240g) icing sugar
20g softened butter
2 tablespoons lemon juice, approximately

1 Preheat oven to 160°C/140°C fan-forced. Grease 8-hole (¾-cup/ 180ml) petite loaf pan.
2 Stir ingredients in large bowl with wooden spoon until combined.
3 Spoon mixture into pan holes, smooth tops; bake about 30 minutes. Stand cakes 5 minutes; turn, top-side up, onto wire rack to cool.
4 Meanwhile, make lemon glacé icing. Drizzle icing over cakes.
lemon glacé icing Sift icing sugar into small heatproof bowl; stir in butter and enough juice to make a firm paste. Stir over small saucepan of simmering water until icing is pourable.

prep + cook time 55 minutes **makes** 8

rhubarb custard tea cake

200g butter, softened
½ cup (110g) caster sugar
2 eggs
1¼ cups (185g) self-raising flour
⅓ cup (40g) custard powder
4 fresh rhubarb stalks (300g),
    sliced lengthways, then
    cut into 10cm lengths
20g butter, melted
2 teaspoons caster sugar, extra

custard
2 tablespoons custard powder
¼ cup (55g) caster sugar
1 cup (250ml) milk
20g butter
2 teaspoons vanilla extract

1 Make custard.
2 Preheat oven to 180°C/160°C fan-forced. Grease deep 20cm-round cake pan; line base with baking paper.
3 Beat softened butter and sugar in small bowl with electric mixer until light and fluffy. Beat in eggs, one at a time. Transfer to medium bowl; stir in sifted flour and custard powder.
4 Spread half the mixture into pan; spread over custard. Dollop small spoonfuls of remaining cake mixture over custard; carefully spread with spatula to completely cover custard. Top cake mixture with rhubarb; brush gently with melted butter then sprinkle with extra sugar.
5 Bake cake about 1¼ hours; cool in pan.
custard Combine custard powder and sugar in small saucepan; gradually stir in milk. Cook, stirring, until mixture boils and thickens slightly. Remove from heat; stir in butter and extract. Press plastic wrap over surface of custard to prevent a skin forming; cool. Whisk until smooth before using.

prep + cook time 1 hour 50 minutes (+ cooling) **serves** 8

ginger cake with caramel icing

¾ cup (165g) firmly packed brown sugar
¾ cup (110g) plain flour
½ cup (75g) self-raising flour
½ teaspoon bicarbonate of soda
2 teaspoons ground ginger
1 teaspoon ground cinnamon
½ teaspoon ground nutmeg
125g butter, softened
2 eggs
⅔ cup (160ml) buttermilk
caramel icing
60g butter
½ cup (110g) firmly packed brown sugar
2 tablespoons milk
¾ cup (120g) icing sugar

1 Preheat oven to 170°C/150°C fan-forced. Grease deep 20cm ring pan.
2 Sift dry ingredients into medium bowl. Add remaining ingredients; beat with electric mixer on low speed until ingredients are combined. Increase speed to medium; beat about 2 minutes or until mixture is smooth and paler in colour.
3 Pour mixture into pan; bake about 35 minutes. Stand cake in pan 10 minute; turn, top-side up, onto wire rack to cool.
4 Meanwhile, make caramel icing. Drizzle warm icing over cake.
caramel icing Stir butter, brown sugar and milk in small saucepan over heat until sugar dissolves; bring to the boil. Reduce heat; simmer, stirring, 2 minutes. Remove from heat; stir in sifted icing sugar.

prep + cook time 1 hour 5 minutes **serves** 10

blueberry yogurt loaf

150g butter, softened
2 teaspoons finely grated lemon rind
1 1/4 cups (275g) firmly packed brown sugar
2 eggs
1 1/4 cups (185g) plain flour
1/2 cup (75g) self-raising flour
2/3 cup (190g) greek-style yogurt
150g frozen blueberries

1 Preheat oven to 170°C/150°C fan-forced. Grease 12cm x 22cm loaf pan; line base and long sides with baking paper, extending paper 5cm over sides.
2 Beat butter, rind and sugar in small bowl with electric mixer until light and fluffy. Beat in eggs, one at a time. Transfer to large bowl; stir in sifted flours and yogurt, in two batches. Fold in blueberries.
3 Spread mixture into pan; bake 1 1/2 hours. Stand cake in pan 5 minutes; turn, top-side up, onto wire rack to cool.

prep + cook time 2 hours **serves** 12

apple raspberry bread

375ml jar apple sauce
1 cup (220g) firmly packed dark brown sugar
2 eggs
40g butter, melted
½ cup (125ml) buttermilk
¼ cup (90g) honey
1½ cups (225g) plain flour
⅔ cup (100g) wholemeal self-raising flour
½ teaspoon bicarbonate of soda
250g fresh or frozen raspberries

1 Preheat oven to 170°C/150°C fan-forced. Grease 12cm x 22cm loaf pan; line base and long sides with baking paper, extending paper 5cm over sides.
2 Combine apple sauce, sugar, eggs, butter, buttermilk and honey in large bowl; stir in sifted dry ingredients. Do not overmix; mixture should be lumpy. Fold in raspberries.
3 Spread mixture into pan; bake about 1 hour 40 minutes. Stand bread in pan 10 minutes; turn, top-side up, onto wire rack to cool.

prep + cook time 1 hour 55 minutes **serves** 12

caramelised apple tea cakes

125g butter, softened
1 teaspoon vanilla extract
⅔ cup (150g) caster sugar
2 eggs
1¼ cups (185g) self-raising flour
½ cup (75g) plain flour
1 teaspoon mixed spice
½ teaspoon ground cinnamon
1 cup (250ml) buttermilk
1 large apple (200g), peeled,
  grated coarsely

caramelised apples
2 small apples (260g)
75g butter
⅓ cup (75g) firmly packed
  brown sugar

1 Make caramelised apples.
2 Preheat oven to 180°C/160°C fan-forced. Grease two six-hole (¾-cup/180ml) texas muffin pans.
3 Place one slice caramelised apple in each pan hole; spoon caramel sauce over apple.
4 Beat butter, extract and sugar in small bowl with electric mixer until light and fluffy. Beat in eggs, one at a time. Transfer to large bowl; stir in sifted dry ingredients and buttermilk, in two batches. Stir in apple.
5 Spoon mixture among pan holes; bake about 30 minutes. Stand cakes in pans 5 minutes; turn, top-side up, onto wire rack. Serve cakes warm.
caramelised apples Slice each unpeeled apple into six 1cm-thick slices. Stir butter and sugar in large frying pan over low heat until sugar dissolves. Add apple slices to caramel sauce; cook, turning occasionally, about 3 minutes or until browned lightly.

prep + cook time 1 hour 10 minutes **makes** 12

raisin and honey oat bread

1¾ cups (260g) self-raising flour
½ cup (110g) firmly packed brown sugar
⅔ cup (60g) rolled oats
1 cup (180g) raisins
2 eggs
½ cup (125ml) buttermilk
½ cup (125ml) vegetable oil
¼ cup (90g) honey

1 Preheat oven to 180°C/160°C fan-forced. Grease 12cm x 22cm loaf pan; line base and long sides with baking paper, extending paper 5cm over sides.
2 Sift flour into large bowl; stir in sugar, oats and raisins. Add eggs, buttermilk, oil and honey; stir to combine.
3 Spread mixture into pan; bake about 1 hour. Stand loaf in pan 10 minutes; turn, top-side up, onto wire rack to cool.

prep + cook time 1 hour 15 minutes **serves** 10

date and pecan roll

30g butter
½ cup (125ml) boiling water
½ cup (90g) finely chopped dried seeded dates
¼ teaspoon bicarbonate of soda
½ cup (110g) firmly packed brown sugar
1 cup (150g) self-raising flour
¼ cup (30g) coarsely chopped pecans
1 egg

1 Adjust oven shelves to fit upright nut roll tin. Preheat oven to
170°C/150°C fan-forced. Grease lids and inside of 8cm x 20cm
nut roll tin evenly with melted butter; place base lid on tin, position tin
upright on oven tray.
2 Stir butter and the water in medium saucepan over low heat until
butter melts. Remove from heat; stir in dates and soda, then remaining
ingredients. Spoon mixture into tin, tap tin firmly on bench to remove
air pockets; position top lid.
3 Bake roll about 1 hour. Stand roll in tin 5 minutes; remove lids
(top and bottom). Shake gently to release roll onto wire rack to cool.
Serve sliced, warm or cold, with butter.

prep + cook time 1 hour 15 minutes **serves** 10
tip Tall 850ml (8cm x 17cm) fruit juice cans make good nut roll tins.
Use a can opener that cuts just below the rims to cut one end from the
can. Wash and dry the can thoroughly before greasing. Use a double-
thickness of foil to cover top of the can and secure with string; slash a
hole in the foil top to allow steam to escape during baking.

fig jam and raisin rolls

125g butter
½ cup (100g) firmly packed brown sugar
2 eggs
1½ cups (225g) self-raising flour
½ cup (160g) fig jam
1 cup (170g) chopped raisins
½ cup (125ml) milk

1 Adjust oven shelves to fit upright nut roll tin. Preheat oven to 200°C/180°C fan forced. Grease lids and inside of two 8cm x 20cm nut roll tins; line bases with baking paper. Place tins upright on oven tray.
2 Beat butter and sugar in small bowl with electric mixer until light and fluffy. Beat in eggs, one at a time. Transfer to medium bowl; stir in flour, jam, raisins and milk, in two batches.
3 Spoon mixture into tin, tap tin firmly on bench to remove air pockets; replace lids. Bake rolls about 50 minutes. Stand rolls in tins 5 minutes; remove lids (top and bottom), shake tins gently to release rolls onto wire rack to cool.

prep + cook time 1 hour 10 minutes **serves** 20 (makes 2 rolls)
tip Tall 850ml (8cm x 17cm) fruit juice cans make good nut roll tins. Use a can opener that cuts just below the rims to cut one end from the can. Wash and dry the can thoroughly before greasing. Use a double-thickness of foil to cover top of the can and secure with string; slash a hole in the foil top to allow steam to escape during baking.

upside down pear and pistachio cake

¼ cup (35g) coarsely chopped unsalted pistachios
1 cup (220g) firmly packed brown sugar
1 large pear (330g), unpeeled, cored, sliced thinly
185g butter, softened
3 eggs
¼ cup (35g) plain flour
1¾ cups (210g) ground almonds

1 Preheat oven to 200°C/180°C fan-forced. Grease shallow 22cm-round cake pan; line base with baking paper.
2 Combine nuts and 2 tablespoons of the sugar in small bowl; sprinkle over base of pan, top with pear slices.
3 Beat butter and remaining sugar in small bowl with electric mixer until light and fluffy. Beat in eggs, one at a time. Stir in sifted flour and ground almonds.
4 Pour mixture into pan; bake about 35 minutes. Stand cake in pan 10 minutes; turn, top-side down, onto wire rack. Serve cake warm or cold.

prep + cook time 50 minutes **serves** 8

raspberry swirl cake

250g butter, softened
1 teaspoon vanilla extract
1¼ cups (275g) caster sugar
3 eggs
2¼ cups (335g) self-raising flour
¾ cup (180ml) milk
150g frozen raspberries, partly thawed
butter frosting
100g butter, softened
1 cup (160g) icing sugar
1 tablespoon milk
pink food colouring

1 Preheat oven to 180°C/160°C fan-forced. Grease deep 23cm-round cake pan; line base and side with baking paper.
2 Beat butter, extract and sugar in medium bowl with electric mixer until light and fluffy. Beat in eggs, one at a time. Stir in sifted flour and milk, in two batches.
3 Divide mixture between two small bowls. Lightly crush raspberries in another small bowl with fork; gently stir crushed raspberries into one bowl of cake mixture. Drop alternate spoonfuls of mixtures into pan. Pull skewer back and forth through cake mixture for a marbled effect.
4 Bake cake about 1 hour. Stand cake in pan 5 minutes; turn, top-side up, onto wire rack to cool.
5 Meanwhile, make butter frosting. Spread plain frosting over cake; dollop cake with spoonfuls of pink frosting, swirl frosting for a marbled effect.
butter frosting Beat butter in small bowl with electric mixer until as white as possible; beat in sifted icing sugar and milk, in two batches. Divide frosting between two small bowls; tint one bowl of frosting pink.

prep + cook time 1 hour 30 minutes **serves** 12

cream cheese fruit cake

You need about 2 medium carrots (240g) to get the required
amount of grated carrot.

100g soft cream cheese
50g butter, softened
½ cup (110g) caster sugar
2 tablespoons golden syrup
2 teaspoons finely grated orange rind
2 eggs
1 cup coarsely grated carrot
¾ cup (180g) chopped mixed glacé fruit
⅔ cup (100g) plain flour
⅔ cup (100g) self-raising flour
⅓ cup (80ml) orange juice

1 Preheat oven to 180°C/160°C fan-forced. Grease deep 20cm ring pan.
2 Beat cream cheese, butter, sugar, syrup and rind in large bowl with
electric mixer until light and fluffy. Beat in eggs, one at a time. Stir in
remaining ingredients.
3 Spread mixture into pan; bake about 50 minutes. Stand cake in pan
15 minutes; turn, top-side up, onto wire rack to cool.

prep + cook time 1 hour 10 minutes **serves** 10

carrot cake with lemon cream cheese frosting

You need about 3 large carrots (540g) to get the required amount of grated carrot.

1 cup (250ml) vegetable oil
1⅓ cups (295g) firmly packed brown sugar
3 eggs
3 cups firmly packed, coarsely grated carrot
1 cup (110g) coarsely chopped walnuts
2½ cups (375g) self-raising flour
½ teaspoon bicarbonate of soda
2 teaspoons mixed spice
lemon cream cheese frosting
30g butter, softened
80g cream cheese, softened
1 teaspoon finely grated lemon rind
1½ cups (240g) icing sugar

1 Preheat oven to 180°C/160°C fan-forced. Grease deep 22cm-round cake pan; line base with baking paper.
2 Beat oil, sugar and eggs in small bowl with electric mixer until thick and creamy. Transfer mixture to large bowl; using wooden spoon, stir in carrot and nuts then sifted dry ingredients.
3 Pour mixture into pan; bake about 1¼ hours. Stand cake in pan 5 minutes; turn, top-side up, onto wire rack to cool.
4 Meanwhile, make lemon cream cheese frosting. Spread top of cold cake with frosting.
lemon cream cheese frosting Beat butter, cream cheese and rind in small bowl with electric mixer until light and fluffy; gradually beat in icing sugar.

prep + cook time 1 hour 40 minutes (+ cooling) **serves** 12

rock cakes

2 cups (300g) self-raising flour
¼ teaspoon ground cinnamon
⅓ cup (75g) caster sugar
90g butter, chopped
1 cup (160g) sultanas
1 egg, beaten lightly
½ cup (125ml) milk
1 tablespoon caster sugar, extra

1 Preheat oven to 200°C/180°C fan-forced. Grease oven trays.
2 Sift flour, cinnamon and sugar into medium bowl; rub in butter.
Stir in sultanas, egg and milk. Do not overmix.
3 Drop rounded tablespoons of mixture about 5cm apart onto trays;
sprinkle with extra sugar.
4 Bake rock cakes about 15 minutes; cool on trays.

prep + cook time 30 minutes **makes** 18
tip Rock cakes can be stored in an airtight container for up to 2 days.

rich fruit cake

3 cups (500g) sultanas
1½ cups (225g) raisins,
  chopped coarsely
¾ cup (120g) dried currants
⅔ cup (110g) mixed peel
1 cup (200g) glacé cherries,
  halved
2 tablespoons marmalade
¾ cup (180ml) dark rum
250g butter, softened
1 teaspoon finely grated
  orange rind

1 teaspoon finely grated
  lemon rind
1 cup (220g) firmly packed
  brown sugar
4 eggs
2 cups (300g) plain flour
½ teaspoon bicarbonate of soda
2 teaspoons mixed spice
2 tablespoons orange marmalade,
  extra, warmed, strained
400g ready-made white icing

1 Combine fruit, marmalade and ½ cup of the rum in large bowl. Cover; stand overnight.
2 Preheat oven to 150°C/130°C fan-forced. Line six deep 10cm-round cake pans with three thicknesses of baking paper, extending paper 5cm above sides.
3 Beat butter, rinds and sugar in small bowl with electric mixer until combined. Beat in eggs, one at a time. Stir butter mixture into fruit mixture; stir in sifted dry ingredients.
4 Spoon mixture evenly into pans; bake about 1½ hours. Brush hot cakes with remaining rum; cover with foil, cool in pans overnight.
5 Brush tops of cakes with extra marmalade. Roll out ready-made icing until 8mm thick. Cut out six 10cm flower shapes from icing; place one shape on top of each cake, smooth surface.

prep + cook time 2 hours 20 minutes (+ standing & cooling) **makes** 6
tip Cake mixture can be baked in these well-buttered pans:
12-hole ¾-cup (180ml) texas muffin pan: bake 1¼ hours
14-hole ¾-cup (180ml) petite loaf pan: bake 1 hour
20-hole ½-cup (125ml) oval friand pan: bake 50 minutes

rich chocolate fruit cake

2 x 425g cans seeded black
  cherries in syrup
1 cup (150g) raisins, chopped
¾ cup (120g) finely chopped
  seeded dried dates
½ cup (80g) sultanas
½ cup (95g) finely chopped
  seeded prunes
1 cup (200g) dried figs,
  chopped finely
1 cup (250ml) marsala
1 cup (120g) pecans
185g butter, softened
2 teaspoons finely grated
  orange rind

1¼ cups (275g) firmly packed
  dark brown sugar
3 eggs
1¼ cups (185g) plain flour
½ cup (75g) self-raising flour
2 tablespoons cocoa powder
2 teaspoons mixed spice
100g dark eating chocolate,
  chopped finely
ganache
200g dark eating chocolate,
  chopped coarsely
½ cup (125ml) cream

1 Drain cherries; reserve ⅓ cup syrup. Quarter cherries. Combine cherries with remaining fruit, ¾ cup of the marsala and reserved cherry syrup in large bowl. Cover; stand overnight.
2 Preheat oven to 150°C/130°C fan-forced. Line deep 22cm-round cake pan with two thicknesses of baking paper, extending paper 5cm above side.
3 Process half the nuts until ground finely; chop remaining nuts coarsely.
4 Beat butter, rind and sugar in small bowl with electric mixer until combined. Beat in eggs, one at a time. Stir egg mixture into fruit mixture; stir in sifted dry ingredients, chocolate and ground and chopped nuts.
5 Spread mixture into pan; bake about 3 hours. Brush hot cake with remaining marsala; cover with foil, cool in pan overnight.
6 Make ganache. Spread cake with ganache; top with chocolate decoration. Dust with sifted icing sugar to serve, if you like.
ganache Stir ingredients in small saucepan over low heat until smooth. Refrigerate, stirring occasionally, about 20 minutes or until spreadable.

prep + cook time 3 hours 50 minutes (+ standing & refrigeration)
serves 20
tip We painted a branch of real holly roughly with melted dark chocolate to make the inedible decoration on the cake.

gluten-free fruit cake

1 ¼ cups (200g) sultanas
1 cup (150g) finely chopped seeded dried dates
1 cup (150g) raisins, chopped coarsely
¾ cup (120g) dried currants
1 cup (250g) coarsely chopped glacé apricot
1 cup (250ml) tokay
185g dairy-free margarine
1 cup (220g) firmly packed dark brown sugar
3 eggs
1 cup (120g) ground almonds
1 ½ cups (270g) rice flour
1 teaspoon cream of tartar
½ teaspoon bicarbonate of soda
1 teaspoon ground nutmeg
½ teaspoon ground ginger
½ teaspoon ground cloves

1 Combine fruit and ¾ cup of the tokay in large bowl. Cover with plastic wrap; stand overnight.
2 Preheat oven to 120°C/100°C fan-forced. Line deep 22cm-round cake pan with two thicknesses of baking paper, extending paper 5cm above side.
3 Beat margarine and sugar in small bowl with electric mixer until combined. Beat in eggs, one at a time. Stir egg mixture into fruit mixture; stir in ground almonds and sifted dry ingredients.
4 Spread mixture into pan; bake about 2½ hours. Brush hot cake with remaining tokay; cover tightly with foil, cool in pan overnight. Serve dusted with sifted pure icing sugar, if you like.

prep + cook time 3 hours (+ standing & cooling) **serves** 20
tips Store cake in the refrigerator for up to three months. Cut the cake straight from the fridge, then bring to room temperature before serving. Tokay is a sweet white fortified wine.

celebration fruit cake

3 cups (500g) sultanas
1¾ cups (300g) raisins, halved
1¾ cups (300g) dried dates, chopped finely
1 cup (150g) dried currants
⅔ cup (110g) mixed peel
⅔ cup (150g) glacé cherries, halved
¼ cup (55g) coarsely chopped glacé pineapple
¼ cup (60g) coarsely chopped glacé apricots
½ cup (125ml) dark rum
250g butter, softened
1 cup (220g) firmly packed brown sugar
5 eggs
1½ cups (225g) plain flour
⅓ cup (50g) self-raising flour
1 teaspoon mixed spice
2 tablespoons dark rum, extra

1 Combine fruit and rum in large bowl. Cover tightly with plastic wrap; stand overnight (or up to a week in a cool, dark place, stirring every day).
2 Preheat oven to 150°C/130°C fan-forced. Line deep 22cm-round cake pan with three thicknesses of baking paper, extending paper 5cm above side.
3 Beat butter and sugar in small bowl with electric mixer until just combined. Beat in eggs, one at a time. Stir egg mixture into fruit mixture; stir in sifted dry ingredients.
4 Spread mixture into pan; bake about 3½ hours. Brush hot cake with extra rum; cover tightly with foil, cool in pan overnight.

prep + cook time 3 hours 50 minutes (+ standing & cooling)
serves 20

lemon currant loaf

125g butter, softened
1 cup (220g) caster sugar
2 teaspoons finely grated lemon rind
3 eggs
1 cup (150g) self-raising flour
½ cup (75g) plain flour
⅓ cup (80g) sour cream
2 tablespoons lemon juice
1 cup (160g) dried currants

1 Preheat oven to 180°C/160°C fan-forced. Grease 12cm x 22cm loaf pan; line base and long sides with baking paper, extending paper 5cm over sides.
2 Beat butter, sugar and rind in medium bowl with electric mixer until light and fluffy. Beat in eggs, one at a time. Stir in sifted flours, sour cream and juice, in two batches. Stir in currants.
3 Spread mixture into pan; bake about 1 hour 10 minutes. Stand loaf in pan 10 minutes; turn, top-side up, onto wire rack to cool.

prep + cook time 1 hour 30 minutes **serves** 10

night-before-christmas fruit cake

You need about 1 large overripe banana (230g) to get the required amount of mashed banana.

1½ cups (240g) mixed dried fruit
⅓ cup (60g) finely chopped glacé ginger
410g jar fruit mince
175g butter, chopped coarsely
⅔ cup (150g) firmly packed brown sugar
1 teaspoon finely grated lemon rind
2 tablespoons lemon juice
½ cup (125ml) brandy
½ teaspoon bicarbonate of soda
3 eggs, beaten lightly
½ cup (140g) mashed banana
1½ cups (225g) plain flour
½ cup (75g) self-raising flour
½ cup (70g) slivered almonds

1 Stir fruit, ginger, fruit mince, butter, sugar, rind, juice and ⅓ cup of the brandy in medium saucepan over heat until butter is melted and sugar dissolved. Bring to the boil. Remove from heat; stir in soda. Transfer to large bowl; cool.
2 Preheat oven to 160°C/140°C fan-forced. Grease 32cm x 22cm rectangular slice pan; line base and two long sides with baking paper, extending paper 5cm above sides.
3 Stir eggs and banana into fruit mixture, then sifted dry ingredients. Spread mixture into pan; sprinkle with nuts.
4 Bake cake about 55 minutes. Brush hot cake with remaining brandy; cover tightly with foil, cool in pan overnight. Cut cake into 25 squares. Dust cakes with sifted icing sugar to serve, if you like.

prep + cook time 1 hour 15 minutes (+ cooling) **serves** 25

rich fruit cake with stout

500g (3 cups) mixed dried fruit
1⅔ cups (100g) coarsely chopped dried apple
⅔ cup (100g) coarsely chopped dried peaches
½ cup (85g) coarsely chopped dried figs
200g butter, chopped coarsely
¾ cup (165g) firmly packed brown sugar
375ml stout
4 eggs
1½ cups (225g) plain flour
½ cup (75g) self-raising flour
½ teaspoon bicarbonate of soda
1 teaspoon mixed spice
½ cup (60g) pecans

1 Grease deep 23cm-round cake pan; line base and side with three thicknesses of baking paper, extending paper 5cm above edge.
2 Stir fruit, butter, sugar and stout in large saucepan over medium heat until sugar dissolves; bring to the boil. Transfer fruit mixture to large heatproof bowl; cool.
3 Preheat oven to 150°C/130°C fan-forced.
4 Stir eggs and sifted dry ingredients into fruit mixture. Spread mixture into pan; decorate with nuts.
5 Bake cake about 2½ hours. Cover hot cake with foil; cool cake in pan overnight.

prep + cook time 2 hours 45 minutes (+ cooling) **serves** 16

orange, almond and pine nut cake

2 medium oranges (480g)
1 teaspoon baking powder
6 eggs
1 cup (220g) caster sugar
2 cups (240g) ground almonds
½ cup (75g) plain flour
⅓ cup (50g) pine nuts

1 Place unpeeled whole oranges in medium saucepan, cover with cold water; bring to the boil. Boil, covered, 1½ hours or until oranges are tender; drain. Cool.
2 Preheat oven to 180°C/160°C fan-forced. Grease deep 23cm-round cake pan; line base and side with baking paper.
3 Trim and discard ends from oranges. Halve oranges; discard seeds. Blend or process oranges, including rind, with baking powder until mixture is pulpy.
4 Beat eggs and sugar in medium bowl with electric mixer about 5 minutes or until thick and creamy. Fold in ground almonds, sifted flour and orange pulp.
5 Pour mixture into pan, sprinkle with nuts; bake about 1 hour. Cool cake in pan.

prep + cook time 3 hours (+ cooling) **serves** 16

SYRUP CAKES

macaroon syrup cake

125g butter, softened
1 cup (220g) caster sugar
4 eggs
2 cups (160g) desiccated coconut
1 cup (150g) self-raising flour
lemon syrup
1 cup (220g) sugar
⅔ cup (160ml) water
6 strips lemon rind

1 Preheat oven to 180°C/160°C fan-forced. Grease deep 20cm ring cake pan; line base and side with baking paper.
2 Beat butter and sugar in medium bowl with electric mixer until light and fluffy. Beat in eggs, one at a time. Stir in coconut, then sifted flour.
3 Spread mixture into pan; bake about 45 minutes.
4 Meanwhile, make lemon syrup. Pour hot syrup over hot cake in pan; cool in pan. Decorate with toasted flaked coconut, if you like.
lemon syrup Stir ingredients in small saucepan over heat without boiling until sugar is dissolved; bring to the boil. Reduce heat; simmer, uncovered, without stirring 3 minutes. Strain syrup.

prep + cook time 1 hour **serves** 10

lime coconut syrup cake

125g butter, softened
1 tablespoon finely grated lime rind
1 cup (220g) caster sugar
3 eggs
1¾ cups (260g) self-raising flour
1 cup (90g) desiccated coconut
½ cup (125ml) yogurt
½ cup (125ml) milk
lime syrup
¾ cup (165g) caster sugar
⅓ cup (80ml) lime juice
¼ cup (60ml) water

1 Preheat oven to 180°C/160°C fan-forced. Grease 20cm baba pan thoroughly (or grease deep 20cm-round cake pan and line base and side with baking paper).
2 Beat butter, rind and sugar in medium bowl with electric mixer until light and fluffy. Beat in eggs, one at a time. Stir in sifted flour and remaining ingredients, in two batches.
3 Spread mixture into pan; bake about 45 minutes. Stand cake in pan 5 minutes; turn onto wire rack over tray.
4 Meanwhile, make lime syrup. Pour hot syrup over hot cake.
lime syrup Stir ingredients in small saucepan over low heat, without boiling, until sugar dissolves. Simmer, uncovered, without stirring, 3 minutes.

prep + cook time 1 hour 15 minutes **serves** 8

caramel cake with whole-spice syrup

185g butter, softened
¾ cup (150g) firmly packed
   brown sugar
⅓ cup (80ml) golden syrup
2 eggs
⅓ cup (40g) ground almonds
½ cup (125ml) milk
2 cups (300g) self-raising flour
1 teaspoon ground cinnamon
1 teaspoon ground nutmeg
1 teaspoon ground ginger

whole-spice syrup
1 medium lemon (140g)
¾ cup (165g) caster sugar
¼ cup (60ml) water
4 cardamom pods, crushed
1 cinnamon stick
1 vanilla bean, split

1 Preheat oven to 180°C/160°C fan-forced. Grease 20cm baba pan
(or grease deep 20cm-round cake pan and line base and side with
baking paper).
2 Beat ingredients in medium bowl with electric mixer on low speed
until ingredients are combined. Increase speed to medium; beat about
5 minutes or until mixture is pale and thick.
3 Spread mixture into pan; bake about 1 hour. Stand cake in pan 5 minutes;
turn onto wire rack set over tray.
4 Meanwhile, make whole-spice syrup. Pour hot syrup over hot cake;
discard whole spices. Serve cake warm or cold.
whole-spice syrup Using a vegetable peeler, remove thin slices lemon
rind; cut slices into 1cm strips. Squeeze lemon; reserve ⅓ cup juice. Stir
rind and juice with remaining ingredients in medium saucepan over low
heat, without boiling, until sugar dissolves. Simmer, uncovered, without
stirring, 3 minutes; transfer to heatproof jug.

prep + cook time 1 hour 20 minutes **serves** 10

semolina and yogurt lemon-syrup cake

250g butter
1 tablespoon finely grated lemon rind
1 cup (220g) caster sugar
3 eggs, separated
1 cup (150g) self-raising flour
1 cup (160g) semolina
1 cup (280g) yogurt
lemon syrup
1 cup (220g) caster sugar
⅓ cup (80ml) lemon juice

1 Preheat oven to 180°C/160°C fan-forced. Grease 20cm baba pan thoroughly (or grease deep 20cm-round cake pan and line base and side with baking paper).
2 Beat butter, rind and sugar in small bowl with electric mixer until light and fluffy. Beat in egg yolks. Transfer mixture to large bowl; stir in sifted flour, semolina and yogurt.
3 Beat egg whites in small bowl with electric mixer until soft peaks form; fold egg whites, into cake mixture, in two batches.
4 Spread mixture into pan; bake about 50 minutes.
5 Meanwhile, make lemon syrup.
6 Stand cake in pan 5 minutes; turn onto wire rack set over tray. Pierce cake all over with skewer; pour hot syrup over hot cake.
lemon syrup Stir ingredients in small saucepan over low heat until sugar dissolves. Bring to the boil, without stirring; remove from heat.

prep + cook time 1 hour 10 minutes **serves** 8

orange and blueberry syrup cake

125g butter, softened
½ cup (110g) caster sugar
2 eggs
1¾ cups (260g) self-raising flour
½ cup (125ml) yogurt
¼ cup (60ml) orange juice
1 cup (150g) frozen blueberries
1 tablespoon finely grated orange rind
orange syrup
¾ cup (165g) caster sugar
½ cup (125ml) orange juice
¼ cup (60ml) water
1 tablespoon grated orange rind

1 Preheat oven to 180°C/160°C fan-forced. Grease deep 20cm ring cake pan; line base and side with baking paper.
2 Beat butter and sugar in medium bowl with electric mixer until light and fluffy. Beat in eggs, one at a time. Stir in flour and combined yogurt and juice, in two batches. Stir in blueberries and rind until just combined.
3 Spread mixture into pan; bake about 1 hour. Stand cake in pan 5 minutes; turn onto wire rack over tray.
4 Meanwhile, make orange syrup. Pour hot syrup over hot cake.
orange syrup Stir sugar, juice and the water in small saucepan over heat, without boiling, until sugar dissolves. Stir in rind; simmer, uncovered, without stirring, 5 minutes.

prep + cook time 1 hour 20 minutes **serves** 10

cinnamon and walnut syrup cake

3 eggs
¾ cup (165g) caster sugar
¾ cup (110g) self-raising flour
3 teaspoons ground cinnamon
185g butter, melted
¾ cup (80g) coarsely chopped walnuts
sugar syrup
1 cup (220) caster sugar
¾ cup (180ml) water

1 Preheat oven to 180°C/160°C fan-forced. Grease 23cm-square
slab pan; line base with baking paper.
2 Beat eggs in small bowl with electric mixer until thick and creamy.
Gradually add sugar, beating until dissolved between additions. Beat in
sifted flour and cinnamon, in two batches; beat in butter then stir in nuts.
3 Pour mixture into pan; bake about 30 minutes. Stand cake in pan
5 minutes; turn onto wire rack set over tray.
4 Meanwhile, make sugar syrup. Pour hot syrup over hot cake. Serve
cake warm or cold.
sugar syrup Stir ingredients in small saucepan over heat without
boiling until sugar is dissolved. Bring to the boil. Reduce heat; simmer,
uncovered, 5 minutes.

prep + cook time 1 hour **serves** 12

orange syrup cake

1 large orange (300g)
2 cups (500ml) water
2 cups (440g) caster sugar
⅔ cup (160ml) brandy
250g unsalted butter, softened
1 cup (220g) caster sugar, extra
4 eggs
1½ cups (225g) self-raising flour
2 tablespoons cornflour

1 Preheat oven to 160°C/140°C fan-forced. Grease deep 22cm round cake pan; line base and side with baking paper.
2 Peel orange. Chop both the peel and the flesh of orange finely; discard seeds. Place flesh and peel in medium saucepan with the water, sugar and brandy over medium heat; stir until sugar dissolves. Bring to the boil. Reduce heat; simmer, uncovered, about 15 minutes or until orange skin is tender. Strain syrup into heatproof jug; reserve solids, cool.
3 Beat butter and extra sugar in small bowl with electric mixer until light and fluffy. Beat in eggs, one at a time. Transfer to large bowl; stir in combined sifted flour and cornflour, and reserved orange solids.
4 Pour mixture into pan; bake about 50 minutes. Stand cake in pan 5 minutes; turn, top-side up, onto wire rack set over tray.
5 Meanwhile, simmer reserved syrup over heat in small saucepan until thickened slightly. Pour hot syrup over hot cake; serve warm.

prep + cook time 1 hour 35 minutes **serves** 12

orange poppy seed syrup cake

⅓ cup (50g) poppy seeds
¼ cup (60ml) milk
185g butter, softened
1 tablespoon finely grated orange rind
1 cup (220g) caster sugar
3 eggs
1½ cups (225g) self-raising flour
½ cup (75g) plain flour
½ cup (60g) ground almonds
½ cup (125ml) orange juice
orange syrup
1 cup (220g) caster sugar
⅔ cup (160ml) orange juice
⅓ cup (80ml) water

1 Preheat oven to 180°C/160°C fan-forced. Grease deep 22cm-round cake pan; line base and side with baking paper.
2 Combine seeds and milk in small bowl; stand 20 minutes.
3 Meanwhile, beat butter, rind and sugar in small bowl with electric mixer until light and fluffy. Beat in eggs, one at a time. Transfer to large bowl; stir in flours, ground almonds, juice and poppy-seed mixture.
4 Spread mixture into pan; bake about 1 hour. Stand cake in pan 5 minutes; turn, top-side up, onto wire rack set over tray.
5 Meanwhile, make orange syrup. Pour hot syrup over hot cake.
orange syrup Stir ingredients in small saucepan over heat, without boiling, until sugar dissolves. Bring to the boil. Reduce heat; simmer, uncovered, without stirring, 2 minutes. Pour syrup into heatproof jug.

prep + cook time 1 hour 25 minutes (+ standing) **serves** 16

banana butterscotch syrup cake

You need 2 large overripe bananas (460g) to get the required amount of mashed banana.

125g butter, softened
¾ cup (165g) caster sugar
2 eggs
1 cup mashed banana
¾ cup (110g) self-raising flour
¾ cup (110g) plain flour
½ teaspoon bicarbonate of soda
¾ cup (110g) hazelnuts, roasted, chopped finely
butterscotch syrup
½ cup (110g) firmly packed brown sugar
30g butter, chopped
¾ cup (180ml) water

1 Preheat oven to 180°C/160°C fan-forced. Grease deep 19cm-square cake pan; line base with baking paper.
2 Beat butter and sugar in medium bowl with electric mixer until light and fluffy. Beat in eggs, one at a time. Stir in banana, then combined sifted flours and soda, and nuts.
3 Spread mixture into pan; bake about 1 hour.
4 Meanwhile, make butterscotch syrup.
5 Stand cake in pan 5 minutes; turn, top-side up, onto wire rack set over tray. Drizzle hot syrup over hot cake.
butterscotch syrup Stir sugar and butter in small saucepan over low heat until butter melts. Add the water and bring to the boil, stirring; remove from heat.

prep + cook time 1 hour 15 minutes **serves** 12

mixed berry cake with vanilla bean syrup

125g butter, chopped
1 cup (220g) caster sugar
3 eggs
½ cup (75g) plain flour
¼ cup (35g) self-raising flour
½ cup (60g) ground almonds
⅓ cup (80g) sour cream
1½ cups (225g) frozen mixed berries
½ cup (100g) drained canned seeded black cherries
vanilla bean syrup
½ cup (110g) caster sugar
½ cup (125ml) water
2 vanilla beans

1 Preheat oven to 180°C/160°C fan-forced. Grease 20cm baba pan thoroughly (or grease deep 20cm-round cake pan and line base and side with baking paper).
2 Beat butter and sugar in small bowl with electric mixer until light and fluffy. Beat in eggs, one at a time. Transfer mixture to large bowl; stir in sifted flours, ground almonds, sour cream, berries and cherries.
3 Pour mixture into pan; bake about 40 minutes.
4 Meanwhile, make vanilla bean syrup.
5 Stand cake in pan 5 minutes; turn onto wire rack set over tray. Pour hot syrup over hot cake.
vanilla bean syrup Place sugar and the water in small saucepan. Split vanilla beans in half lengthways; scrape seeds into pan then add pods. Stir over heat, without boiling, until sugar dissolves. Simmer, uncovered, without stirring, 5 minutes. Using tongs, remove pods from syrup.

prep + cook time 1 hour **serves** 8

lime and ricotta syrup cake

200g butter, softened
1 tablespoon finely grated lime rind
1 cup (220g) caster sugar
3 eggs, separated
250g ricotta cheese
½ cup (125ml) milk
1½ cups (225g) self-raising flour
lime syrup
⅔ cup (150g) caster sugar
⅓ cup (80ml) lime juice
¼ cup (60ml) water

1 Preheat oven to 180°C/160°C fan-forced. Grease 20cm baba pan thoroughly (or grease deep 20cm-round cake pan and line base and side with baking paper).
2 Beat butter, rind and sugar in small bowl with electric mixer until light and fluffy. Beat in egg yolks, cheese and milk. Transfer to large bowl; stir in sifted flour.
3 Beat egg whites in small bowl with electric mixer until soft peaks form; fold into cheese mixture, in two batches.
4 Spread mixture into pan; bake about 1 hour. Stand cake in pan 5 minutes; turn onto wire rack set over tray.
5 Meanwhile, make lime syrup. Pour hot syrup over hot cake. Serve cake warm, with whipped cream, if you like.
lime syrup Stir ingredients in small saucepan over low heat until sugar dissolves; bring to the boil. Boil, uncovered, 2 minutes or until syrup thickens slightly.

prep + cook time 1 hour 15 minutes **serves** 10

glacé fruit loaf with ginger syrup

185g butter, softened
½ cup (110g) caster sugar
3 eggs
1 cup (250g) finely chopped glacé apricot
½ cup (80g) finely chopped glacé orange
½ cup (90g) finely chopped glacé ginger
¾ cup (210g) finely chopped glacé fig
1½ cups (225g) plain flour
½ cup (75g) self-raising flour
½ cup (125ml) milk
¼ cup (60ml) ginger wine
ginger syrup
¼ cup (60ml) ginger wine
¼ cup (60ml) water
¼ cup (55g) caster sugar
2 teaspoons lemon juice

1 Preheat oven to 150°C/130°C fan-forced. Line base and both long sides of 14cm x 21cm loaf pan with baking paper, extending paper 5cm above sides.
2 Beat butter and sugar in small bowl with electric mixer until just combined. Beat in eggs, one at a time. Transfer mixture to large bowl; stir in fruit then sifted flours, and combined milk and wine, in two batches.
3 Spread mixture into pan; bake about 2 hours 30 minutes.
4 Meanwhile, make ginger syrup. Pour hot syrup over hot cake in pan. Cover cake with foil; cool in pan.
ginger syrup Stir ingredients in small saucepan over low heat, without boiling, until sugar dissolves; bring to the boil. Boil, uncovered, without stirring, about 2 minutes or until syrup thickens slightly.

prep + cook time 2 hours 50 minutes **serves** 12

espresso syrup cake

3 teaspoons instant espresso coffee granules
1 tablespoon hot water
3 eggs
¾ cup (165g) caster sugar
1 cup (150g) self-raising flour
1 tablespoon cocoa powder
150g butter, melted
espresso syrup
¾ cup (165g) caster sugar
¾ cup (180ml) water
3 teaspoons instant espresso coffee granules

1 Preheat oven to 180°C/160°C fan-forced. Grease 20cm baba pan (or grease deep 20cm-round cake pan and line base and side with baking paper).
2 Combine coffee and the water in small jug; stir until dissolved.
3 Beat eggs in small bowl with electric mixer about 8 minutes or until thick and creamy; gradually add sugar, beating until dissolved between additions. Fold in sifted flour and cocoa, then butter and coffee mixture.
4 Pour mixture into pan; bake about 40 minutes. Stand cake in pan 5 minutes; turn onto wire rack set over tray.
5 Meanwhile, make espresso syrup. Reserve ¼ cup espresso syrup; drizzle remaining hot syrup over hot cake. Serve with reserved syrup.
espresso syrup Stir ingredients in small saucepan over heat, without boiling, until sugar dissolves. Bring to the boil; remove from heat.

prep + cook time 1 hour **serves** 10

lemon syrup cake

250g butter, softened
1 tablespoon finely grated lemon rind
1 cup (220g) caster sugar
3 eggs
1 cup (250ml) buttermilk
⅓ cup (80ml) lemon juice
2 cups (300g) self-raising flour
lemon syrup
¾ cup (165g) caster sugar
⅓ cup (80ml) lemon juice
¼ cup (60ml) water

1 Preheat oven to 180°C/160°C fan-forced. Grease 24cm baba pan.
2 Beat butter, rind and sugar in small bowl with electric mixer until light and fluffy. Beat in eggs, one at a time. Transfer to large bowl; fold in buttermilk, juice and sifted flour, in two batches.
3 Spread mixture into pan; bake about 50 minutes (cover cake with foil if browning too quickly). Stand cake in pan 5 minutes; turn onto wire rack set over tray.
4 Meanwhile, make lemon syrup. Pour hot syrup over hot cake; serve warm.
lemon syrup Stir ingredients in small saucepan over heat, without boiling, until sugar dissolves. Simmer, uncovered, without stirring, 5 minutes.

prep + cook time 1 hour 10 minutes **serves** 12

CUPCAKES

banana caramel cupcakes

You need about 2 medium overripe bananas (400g) to get the required amount of mashed banana.

90g butter, softened
½ cup (110g) firmly packed brown sugar
2 eggs
½ cup (75g) self-raising flour
½ cup (75g) plain flour
½ teaspoon bicarbonate of soda
½ teaspoon mixed spice
⅔ cup mashed overripe banana
⅓ cup (80g) sour cream
2 tablespoons milk
380g can top 'n' fill caramel
½ cup (125ml) thickened cream, whipped
2 medium bananas (400g), extra, sliced thinly
100g dark eating chocolate

1 Preheat oven to 180°C/160°C fan-forced. Line 6-hole texas (¾-cup/180ml) muffin pan with paper cases.
2 Beat butter, sugar and eggs in small bowl with electric mixer until light and fluffy. Stir in sifted dry ingredients, mashed banana, sour cream and milk.
3 Spoon mixture into paper cases; smooth surface. Bake cakes about 25 minutes. Turn cakes onto wire rack to cool. Remove cases from cakes.
4 Fold 2 tablespoons of the caramel into cream.
5 Cut cakes horizontally into three slices. Re-assemble cakes with remaining caramel and banana slices. Top cakes with caramel-flavoured cream. Using a vegetable peeler, grate chocolate; sprinkle over cakes.

prep + cook time 55 minutes (+ cooling) **makes** 6
tip This recipe also makes 12 standard muffins (⅓-cup/80ml capacity holes). Bake cakes for 20 minutes.

apple custard teacakes

90g butter
½ teaspoon vanilla extract
½ cup (110g) caster sugar
2 eggs
¾ cup (110g) self-raising flour
¼ cup (30g) custard powder
2 tablespoons milk
1 large unpeeled apple (200g),
    cored, sliced finely
30g butter, extra, melted
1 tablespoon caster sugar, extra
½ teaspoon ground cinnamon

custard
1 tablespoon custard powder
1 tablespoon caster sugar
½ cup (125ml) milk
¼ teaspoon vanilla extract

1 Make custard.
2 Preheat oven to 180°C/160°C fan-forced. Line 6-hole texas (¾-cup/ 180ml) muffin pan with paper cases.
3 Beat butter, extract, sugar, eggs, flour, custard powder and milk in small bowl with electric mixer on low speed until ingredients are just combined. Increase speed to medium; beat until mixture is changed to a paler colour.
4 Spoon half the mixture into paper cases; top with custard, then remaining cake mixture, spreading mixture to cover custard. Top with apple slices, pressing slightly into cake.
5 Bake cakes about 40 minutes. Brush hot cakes with extra butter, then sprinkle with combined extra sugar and cinnamon. Turn cakes onto wire rack. Serve warm or cold.
custard Blend custard powder and sugar with milk and extract in small saucepan; stir over heat until mixture boils and thickens. Remove from heat; cover surface with plastic wrap. Cool.

prep + cook time 55 minutes (+ cooling) **makes** 6
tip This recipe also makes 12 standard muffins (⅓-cup/80ml capacity holes). Bake cakes for 30 minutes.

banana cupcakes with maple cream frosting

60g butter, softened
60g soft cream cheese
¾ cup (165g) firmly packed brown sugar
2 eggs
½ cup (125ml) milk
2 tablespoons maple syrup
1½ cups (225g) self-raising flour
½ teaspoon bicarbonate of soda
2 medium bananas (400g), halved lengthways, sliced thinly
maple cream frosting
30g butter, softened
80g soft cream cheese
2 tablespoons maple syrup
1½ cups (240g) icing sugar

1 Preheat oven to 180°C/160°C fan-forced. Line 12-hole (⅓-cup/80ml) muffin pan with paper cases.
2 Beat butter, cream cheese and sugar in medium bowl with electric mixer until light and fluffy. Beat in eggs, one at a time. Stir in milk, syrup and sifted dry ingredients; fold in bananas.
3 Drop ¼ cups of mixture into each paper case; bake about 30 minutes. Stand cakes in pans 5 minutes; turn, top-side up, onto wire rack to cool.
4 Meanwhile, make maple cream frosting. Spread cakes with frosting.
maple cream frosting Beat butter, cream cheese and syrup in small bowl with electric mixer until light and fluffy. Beat in sifted icing sugar, in two batches, until combined.

prep + cook time 40 minutes **makes** 12

carrot and orange cupcakes

You need about 2 medium carrots (240g) to get the required amount of grated carrot.

⅔ cup (160ml) vegetable oil
¾ cup (165g) firmly packed brown sugar
2 eggs
1 teaspoon finely grated orange rind
1½ cups (210g) firmly packed coarsely grated carrot
1¾ cups (260g) self-raising flour
¼ teaspoon bicarbonate of soda
1 teaspoon mixed spice
orange glacé icing
2 cups (320g) icing sugar
20g butter, melted
2 tablespoons orange juice, approximately

1 Preheat oven to 180°C/160°C fan-forced. Line 12-hole (⅓-cup/80ml) muffin pan with paper cases.
2 Beat oil, sugar, eggs and rind in small bowl with electric mixer until thick and creamy. Transfer mixture to large bowl; stir in carrot, then sifted dry ingredients.
3 Spoon mixture into paper cases; bake about 30 minutes. Stand cakes in pan 5 minutes; turn, top-side up, onto wire rack to cool.
4 Meanwhile, make orange glacé icing. Spread cakes with icing.
orange glacé icing Sift icing sugar into small heatproof bowl; stir in butter and enough juice to make a firm paste. Stir over small saucepan of simmering water until spreadable.

prep + cook time 50 minutes **makes** 12

cloud cupcakes

90g butter, softened
½ teaspoon vanilla extract
½ cup (110g) caster sugar
2 eggs
1 cup (150g) self-raising flour
2 tablespoons milk
2 tablespoons strawberry jam
pink coloured sugar

fluffy frosting
1 cup (220g) caster sugar
⅓ cup (80ml) water
2 egg whites

1 Preheat oven to 180°C/160°C fan-forced. Line 6-hole texas (¾-cup/ 180ml) with paper cases.
2 Beat butter, extract, sugar, eggs, flour and milk in small bowl with electric mixer on low speed until ingredients are just combined. Increase speed to medium, beat until mixture is changed to a paler colour.
3 Spoon mixture into cases; smooth surface. Divide jam over tops of cakes; using a skewer swirl jam into cakes.
4 Bake cakes about 30 minutes. Turn cakes onto wire rack to cool.
5 Meanwhile, make fluffy frosting.
6 Spread cakes with fluffy frosting; sprinkle with coloured sugar.
fluffy frosting Stir sugar and the water in small saucepan over heat, without boiling, until sugar is dissolved. Boil, uncovered, without stirring about 5 minutes or until syrup reaches 116°C on a candy thermometer. Syrup should be thick but not coloured. Remove from heat, allow bubbles to subside. Beat egg whites in small bowl with electric mixer until soft peaks form. While motor is operating, add hot syrup in thin stream; beat on high speed about 10 minutes or until mixture is thick and cool.

prep + cook time 50 minutes (+ cooling) **makes** 6
tips To make coloured sugar, place required amount of granulated or caster sugar (depending on the texture you prefer) in a plastic bag and add a tiny amount of colouring. Work the colouring through the sugar by 'massaging' the plastic bag. Sugar will keep in a jar indefinitely.
This recipe also makes 12 standard muffins (⅓-cup/80ml capacity holes). Bake cakes for 20 minutes.

florentine cupcakes

60g dark eating chocolate,
  chopped coarsely
⅔ cup (160ml) water
90g butter, softened
1 cup (220g) firmly packed
  brown sugar
2 eggs
⅔ cup (100g) self-raising flour
2 tablespoons cocoa powder
⅓ cup (40g) ground almonds
50g dark eating chocolate,
  extra, melted

milk chocolate ganache
100g milk eating chocolate,
  chopped coarsely
¼ cup (60ml) cream
florentine topping
1 cup (80g) flaked almonds,
  roasted
½ cup (115g) coarsely chopped
  glacé ginger
1 cup (200g) red glacé cherries,
  halved

1 Preheat oven to 160°C/140°C fan-forced. Line 6-hole texas
(¾-cup/180ml) muffin pan with paper cases.
2 Stir chocolate and the water in small saucepan over low heat until smooth.
3 Beat butter, sugar and eggs in small bowl with electric mixer until
light and fluffy. Stir in sifted flour and cocoa, ground almonds and warm
chocolate mixture.
4 Spoon mixture into cases; smooth surface. Bake about 35 minutes.
Turn cakes onto wire rack to cool.
5 Meanwhile, make milk chocolate ganache.
6 Make florentine topping.
7 Spread cakes with ganache, top with florentine mixture; drizzle with
melted chocolate.
milk chocolate ganache Place chocolate in small heatproof bowl.
Bring cream to the boil in small saucepan; pour over chocolate, stir
until smooth. Stand at room temperature until ganache is spreadable.
florentine topping Combine ingredients in small bowl.

prep + cook time 50 minutes (+ cooling & standing) **makes** 6
tip This recipe also makes 12 standard muffins (⅓-cup/80ml capacity
holes). Bake cakes for 25 minutes.

chocolate fudge mud cakes

3 x 60g Mars Bars
150g butter, chopped coarsely
150g dark eating chocolate, chopped coarsely
½ cup (110g) firmly packed brown sugar
1 cup (250ml) water
½ cup (75g) plain flour
¼ cup (35g) self-raising flour
2 eggs
chocolate fudge frosting
50g dark eating chocolate, chopped coarsely
25g butter
1 cup (160g) icing sugar
1 tablespoon cocoa powder
2 tablespoons hot water, approximately

1 Preheat oven to 180°C/160°C fan-forced. Grease 12-hole (⅓-cup/ 80ml) muffin pan.
2 Chop two Mars Bars finely; cut remaining bar into 12 slices.
3 Stir butter, chocolate, sugar and the water in medium saucepan over low heat until smooth. Transfer mixture to large bowl; cool 10 minutes. Whisk in sifted flours then eggs and finely chopped Mars Bar.
4 Spoon mixture into pan holes; bake about 25 minutes. Stand cakes in pan 5 minutes; turn, top-side up, onto wire rack to cool.
5 Meanwhile, make chocolate fudge frosting. Spread cakes with frosting; top each with a slice of Mars Bar.
chocolate fudge frosting Stir chocolate and butter in small heatproof bowl over small saucepan of simmering water until smooth (do not allow water to touch base of bowl); stir in sifted icing sugar and cocoa. Stir in enough of the hot water until frosting is spreadable.

prep + cook time 45 minutes **makes** 12

candy cupcakes

80g butter, softened
¼ teaspoon vanilla extract
⅓ cup (75g) caster sugar
2 eggs
1 cup (150g) self-raising flour
2 tablespoons milk
2 x 40g jars mini boiled lollies

1 Preheat oven to 180°C/160°C fan-forced. Line 12-hole (2-tablespoon/40ml) deep flat-based patty pan with paper cases.
2 Beat butter, extract, sugar, eggs, sifted flour and milk in small bowl with electric mixer on low speed until ingredients are combined. Increase speed to medium; beat about 2 minutes or until mixture is smooth and paler in colour.
3 Spoon mixture into paper cases; bake 15 minutes. Remove cakes from oven; sprinkle lollies over cakes. Bake a further 5 minutes or until lollies melt. Stand cakes in pan 5 minutes; turn, top-side up, onto wire rack to cool.

prep + cook time 35 minutes **makes** 12

pineapple hibiscus cupcakes

½ cup (125ml) vegetable oil
3 eggs, beaten lightly
1½ cups (225g) self-raising flour
¾ cup (165g) caster sugar
½ teaspoon ground cinnamon
2 cups (440g) firmly packed
coarsely grated carrot
¾ cup (160g) drained crushed
pineapple

pineapple flowers
1 tablespoon caster sugar
1 tablespoon water
12 wafer thin slices fresh
pineapple
lemon cream cheese frosting
30g butter, softened
80g cream cheese, softened
1 teaspoon finely grated
lemon rind
1½ cups (240g) icing sugar

1 Make pineapple flowers.
2 Preheat oven to 180°C/160°C fan-forced. Line a 6-hole texas
(¾-cup/180ml) muffin pan with paper cases.
3 Combine oil, eggs, flour, sugar and cinnamon in medium bowl.
Stir in carrot and pineapple.
4 Spoon mixture into paper cases; bake about 40 minutes.
Turn cakes onto wire rack to cool.
5 Make lemon cream cheese frosting; spread on top of cakes.
Decorate with pineapple flowers.
pineapple flowers Preheat oven to 120°C/100°C fan-forced. Stir
sugar and the water together in a small saucepan over low heat until
sugar has dissolved; boil 1 minute. Brush both sides of pineapple slices
with sugar syrup. Place slices in a single layer on wire racks over oven
trays. Dry pineapple in oven about 1 hour. Immediately remove slices
from rack; carefully shape into flowers. Dry over an egg carton.
lemon cream cheese frosting Beat butter, cream cheese and rind
in small bowl with electric mixer until light and fluffy; gradually beat in
sifted icing sugar.

prep + cook time 2 hours (+ standing & cooling) **makes** 6
tip This recipe also makes 12 standard muffins (⅓-cup/80ml capacity
holes). Bake cakes for 30 minutes.

sweet violet cupcakes

90g butter, softened
90g cream cheese, softened
2 teaspoons finely grated lemon rind
⅔ cup (150g) caster sugar
2 eggs
⅓ cup (50g) self-raising flour
½ cup (75g) plain flour
tea-lights
fresh violets
lemon cream cheese frosting
30g butter, softened
80g cream cheese, softened
1 teaspoon finely grated lemon rind
1½ cups (240g) icing sugar

1 Preheat oven to 180°C/160°C fan-forced. Line 6-hole texas (¾-cup/180ml) muffin pan with paper cases.
2 Beat butter, cream cheese, rind, sugar and eggs in small bowl with electric mixer until light and fluffy. Add sifted flours; beat on low speed until just combined.
3 Spoon mixture into paper cases; smooth surface. Bake cakes about 35 minutes. Turn cakes onto wire rack to cool.
4 Make lemon cream cheese frosting; spread frosting on top of cakes, decorate with tea-lights and violets.
lemon cream cheese frosting Beat butter, cream cheese and rind in small bowl with electric mixer until light and fluffy; gradually beat in sifted icing sugar.

prep + cook time 55 minutes (+ cooling) **makes** 6
tip This recipe also makes 12 standard muffins (⅓-cup/80ml capacity holes). Bake cakes for 25 minutes.

patty cakes with glacé icing

125g butter, softened
½ teaspoon vanilla extract
¾ cup (165g) caster sugar
3 eggs
2 cups (300g) self-raising flour
¼ cup (60ml) milk

glacé icing
2 cups (320g) icing sugar
20g butter, melted
2 tablespoons hot water,
  approximately

1 Preheat oven to 180°C/160°C fan-forced. Line a 12-hole (⅓-cup/ 80ml) muffin pan with paper cases.
2 Beat ingredients in medium bowl with electric mixer on low speed until ingredients are combined. Increase speed to medium; beat about 3 minutes or until mixture is smooth and paler in colour.
3 Spoon mixture into paper cases; bake about 25 minutes. Stand cakes in pan 5 minutes; turn, top-side up, onto wire racks to cool.
4 Meanwhile, make glacé icing. Spread cool cakes with icing.
glacé icing Sift icing sugar into small heatproof bowl; stir in butter and enough of the water to make a firm paste. Stir over small saucepan of simmering water until icing is spreadable.

cake variations
berry & orange Stir in 1 teaspoon finely grated orange rind and ½ cup dried mixed berries at the end of step 2.
citrus Stir in ½ teaspoon each of finely grated lime, orange and lemon rind at the end of step 2.
passionfruit & white chocolate Stir in ¼ cup passionfruit pulp and ½ cup white Choc Bits at the end of step 2.

icing variations
coconut & lime Stir in ½ teaspoon coconut essence and 1 teaspoon finely grated lime rind.
orange Stir in 1 teaspoon finely grated orange rind. Replace 1 tablespoon of the hot water with orange juice.
passionfruit Stir in 1 tablespoon passionfruit pulp.

prep + cook time 45 minutes **makes** 12

orange blossom cakes

100g butter, softened
1 teaspoon orange blossom water
½ cup (110g) caster sugar
2 eggs
1 cup (150g) self-raising flour
¼ cup (30g) ground almonds
½ cup (125ml) milk
orange blossom glacé icing
1 cup (160g) icing sugar
10g softened butter
1 teaspoon orange blossom water
1 tablespoon water, approximately

1 Preheat oven to 180°C/160°C fan-forced. Grease six-hole (¾-cup/ 180ml) mini fluted tube pan or texas muffin pan.
2 Beat butter, blossom water and sugar in small bowl with electric mixer until light and fluffy. Beat in eggs, one at a time (mixture will curdle). Stir in sifted flour, ground almonds and milk, in two batches.
3 Spoon mixture into pan holes; bake about 25 minutes. Stand cakes in pan 5 minutes; turn, top-side up, onto wire rack to cool.
4 Meanwhile, make orange blossom glacé icing. Drizzle icing over cakes.
orange blossom glacé icing Sift icing sugar into small heatproof bowl; stir in butter, blossom water and enough of the boiling water to make a firm paste. Stir over small saucepan of simmering water until icing is pourable.

prep + cook time 45 minutes **makes** 6
tip Orange blossom water is a concentrated flavouring made from orange blossoms; it is available from Middle-Eastern food stores, some supermarkets and delicatessens. Citrus flavourings are very different.

berry cupcakes

125g butter, softened
½ teaspoon vanilla extract
⅔ cup (150g) caster sugar
2 eggs
1 cup (150g) dried mixed berries
½ cup (70g) slivered almonds
⅔ cup (100g) plain flour
⅓ cup (50g) self-raising flour
¼ cup (60ml) milk

sugared fruit
150g fresh blueberries
120g fresh raspberries
1 egg white, beaten lightly
2 tablespoons vanilla sugar
cream cheese frosting
30g butter, softened
80g cream cheese, softened
1½ cups (240g) icing sugar

1 Prepare sugared fruit.
2 Preheat oven to 160°C/140°C fan-forced. Line 6-hole texas (¾-cup/180ml) muffin pan with paper cases.
3 Beat butter, extract, sugar and eggs in small bowl with electric mixer until light and fluffy. Stir in fruit and nuts, then sifted flours and milk.
4 Spoon mixture into paper cases; smooth surface. Bake cakes about 45 minutes. Turn cakes onto wire rack to cool.
5 Make cream cheese frosting.
6 Spread cakes with frosting. Decorate with sugared fruit.
sugared fruit Brush each berry lightly with egg white; roll fruit in sugar. Place fruit on baking-paper-lined tray. Leave about 1 hour or until sugar is dry.
cream cheese frosting Beat butter and cheese in small bowl with electric mixer until light and fluffy; gradually beat in sifted icing sugar.

prep + cook time 1 hour 15 minutes (+ cooling) **makes** 6
tip This recipe also makes 12 standard muffins (⅓-cup/80ml capacity holes). Bake cakes for 35 minutes.

lemon meringue cupcakes

125g butter, softened
2 teaspoons finely grated
  lemon rind
⅔ cup (150g) caster sugar
2 eggs
⅓ cup (80ml) milk
¾ cup (60g) desiccated coconut
1¼ cups (185g) self-raising flour

lemon curd
4 egg yolks
⅓ cup (75g) caster sugar
2 teaspoons finely grated
  lemon rind
¼ cup (60ml) lemon juice
40g butter
coconut meringue
4 egg whites
1 cup (220g) caster sugar
1⅓ cups (95g) shredded coconut,
  chopped finely

1 Make lemon curd.
2 Preheat oven to 180°C/160°C fan-forced. Line 6-hole texas
(¾-cup/180ml) muffin pan with paper cases.
3 Beat butter, rind, sugar and eggs in small bowl with electric mixer until
light and fluffy. Stir in milk and coconut, then sifted flour.
4 Spoon mixture among cases; smooth surface. Bake about 25 minutes.
Turn cakes onto wire rack to cool. Increase oven to 220°C/200°C fan-forced.
5 Cut a 2cm deep hole in the centre of each cake, fill with curd; discard
cake tops.
6 Make coconut meringue; spoon into a piping bag fitted with a 1cm
plain tube. Pipe meringue on top of each cake; place cakes on oven tray.
7 Bake in hot oven 5 minutes or until meringue is browned lightly.
lemon curd Stir ingredients, constantly, in a small heatproof bowl over
small saucepan of simmering water until mixture thickens slightly and
coats the back of a spoon. Remove from heat. Cover tightly; refrigerate
until cold.
coconut meringue Beat egg whites in small bowl with electric mixer
until soft peaks form; gradually add sugar, beating until sugar dissolves.
Fold in coconut.

prep + cook time 1 hour 10 minutes (+ refrigeration & cooling) **makes** 6
tip This recipe also makes 12 standard muffins (⅓-cup/80ml capacity
holes). Bake cakes for 20 minutes.

raspberry and apple cupcakes

125g butter, softened
1 teaspoon vanilla extract
¾ cup (165g) caster sugar
2 eggs
1½ cups (225g) self-raising flour
½ cup (125ml) milk
150g fresh or frozen raspberries
1 large apple (200g), peeled, chopped finely
2 teaspoons icing sugar

1 Preheat oven to 180°C/160°C fan-forced. Line 12-hole (⅓-cup/80ml) muffin pan with paper cases.
2 Beat butter, extract and sugar in small bowl with electric mixer until light and fluffy. Beat in eggs, one at a time. Stir in sifted flour and milk, in two batches. Stir in raspberries and apple.
3 Spoon mixture into paper cases; bake about 30 minutes. Stand cakes in pan 5 minutes; turn, top-side up, onto wire rack to cool. Dust with sifted icing sugar.

prep + cook time 45 minutes **makes** 12
tip If using frozen raspberries, use them straight from the freezer as thawed berries will bleed colour through the cake mix.

mini butterfly cakes

45g butter, softened
¼ teaspoon vanilla extract
¼ cup (55g) caster sugar
1 egg
½ cup (75g) self-raising flour
1½ tablespoons milk
⅓ cup (25g) desiccated coconut
⅓ cup (80ml) thickened cream, whipped
chocolate icing
½ cup (80g) icing sugar
1 tablespoon cocoa powder
5g softened butter
1 tablespoon milk, approximately

1 Preheat oven to 200°C/180°C fan-forced. Line 18 holes of two 12-hole (1-tablespoon/20ml) mini muffin pans with paper cases.
2 Beat butter, extract, sugar, egg, sifted flour, and milk in small bowl with electric mixer on low speed until ingredients are combined. Increase speed to medium; beat about 2 minutes or until mixture is smooth and paler in colour.
3 Spoon mixture into paper cases; bake about 10 minutes. Stand cakes in pan 5 minutes; turn, top-side up, onto wire rack to cool.
4 Meanwhile, make chocolate icing.
5 Dip cake tops into icing, drain excess icing then dip into coconut. Cut tops from each cake; cut tops in half to make butterfly wings. Spoon cream onto each cake; position wings in cream.
chocolate icing Sift icing sugar and cocoa into medium heatproof bowl; stir in butter and enough of the milk to make a firm paste. Stir over medium saucepan of simmering water until icing is spreadable.

prep + cook time 40 minutes **makes** 18

coconut cherry heart cupcakes

125g butter, softened
½ teaspoon coconut essence
⅔ cup (150g) caster sugar
2 eggs
⅓ cup (80ml) milk
½ cup (40g) desiccated coconut
⅓ cup (70g) red glacé cherries, chopped coarsely
50g dark eating chocolate, chopped coarsely
1 cup (150g) self-raising flour
¼ cup (35g) plain flour
150g white chocolate Melts, melted
pink food colouring
milk chocolate ganache
100g milk eating chocolate, chopped coarsely
¼ cup (60ml) cream

1 Preheat oven to 180°C/160°C fan-forced. Line 6-hole texas (¾-cup/
180ml) muffin pan with paper cases.
2 Beat butter, essence, sugar and eggs in small bowl with electric mixer until
combined. Stir in milk, coconut, cherries and chocolate, then sifted flours.
3 Spoon mixture into paper cases; smooth surface. Bake cakes about
35 minutes. Turn cakes onto wire rack to cool.
4 Make milk chocolate ganache.
5 Divide white chocolate evenly among three small bowls; tint two
portions with two different shades of pink.
6 Using small piping bags; spoon a different coloured chocolate mixture
into each bag. Pipe different coloured heart shapes in varying sizes,
onto baking-paper-lined oven tray. Set at room temperature.
7 Spread cakes with ganache; decorate with coloured hearts.
milk chocolate ganache Place chocolate in small heatproof bowl.
Bring cream to the boil in small saucepan; pour over chocolate, stir until
smooth. Cover; stand at room temperature until ganache is spreadable.

prep + cook time 35 minutes (+ cooling & refrigeration) **makes** 6
tip This recipe also makes 12 standard muffins (⅓-cup/80ml capacity
holes). Bake cakes for 20 minutes.

christmas star cupcakes

1.1kg (4½ cups) fruit mince
185g butter, chopped coarsely
¾ cup (165g) firmly packed
   brown sugar
⅓ cup (80ml) bourbon whiskey
⅓ cup (80ml) water
2 teaspoons finely grated
   orange rind
1 teaspoon finely grated
   lemon rind

1 tablespoon treacle
3 eggs
1¼ cups (185g) plain flour
¼ cup (35g) self-raising flour
½ teaspoon bicarbonate of soda
500g ready-made white icing
100g ready-made almond icing
1 cup (160g) icing sugar
1 egg white

1 Stir fruit mince, butter, brown sugar, whiskey and the water in large
saucepan over heat until butter is melted and sugar dissolved; bring to
the boil. Remove from heat; transfer to large heatproof bowl. Cool.
2 Preheat oven to 150°C/130°C fan-forced. Line 22 holes of two
12-hole (⅓-cup/80ml) muffin pans with paper cases.
3 Stir rinds, treacle and eggs into fruit mixture, then sifted flours and soda.
4 Spoon mixture into paper cases; bake about 40 minutes. Cover; cool
in pan overnight.
5 Trim top of each cake to make it flat. Knead white icing and almond
icing together on bench dusted with some of the sifted icing sugar until
smooth. Roll three-quarters of the icing to 5mm thickness. Cut 22 x
6.5cm rounds from icing; cut a 2cm round from centre of each round.
6 Brush top of each cake with egg white; top with icing rounds. Roll
remaining icing on bench dusted with more sifted icing sugar to 3mm
thickness. Cut out 22 stars using a 4cm cutter and 44 stars using a
1.5cm cutter. Decorate cakes with stars by brushing each with a little
egg white to secure in position.

prep + cook time 1 hour 15 minutes (+ cooling) **makes** 22

turkish delight cupcakes

60g white eating chocolate, chopped roughly
2 tablespoons rose water
½ cup (125ml) water
⅓ cup (45g) pistachios
90g butter, softened
1 cup (220g) firmly packed brown sugar
2 eggs
⅔ cup (100g) self-raising flour
2 tablespoons plain flour
⅔ cup (90g) coarsely chopped pistachios, extra
300g white eating chocolate, extra, melted
900g turkish delight, chopped

1 Preheat oven to 180°C/160°C fan-forced. Line 6-hole texas
(¾-cup/180ml) muffin pan with paper cases.
2 Stir chopped chocolate, rose water and the water in small saucepan
over low heat until smooth.
3 Blend or process pistachios until fine.
4 Beat butter, sugar and eggs in small bowl with electric mixer until
combined. Fold in sifted flours, ground pistachios and chocolate mixture.
5 Spoon mixture into paper cases; bake about 35 minutes. Turn cakes
onto wire rack to cool.
6 Cut a 3cm deep hole in the centre of each cake; fill with a few chopped
pistachios. Drizzle with a little melted chocolate; replace lids. Decorate
cakes with pieces of turkish delight and remaining chopped pistachios
dipped in chocolate.

prep + cook time 55 minutes **makes** 6
tip This recipe also makes 12 standard muffins (⅓-cup/80ml capacity
holes). Bake cakes for 20 minutes.

rocky road cupcakes

125g butter, softened
½ teaspoon vanilla extract
⅔ cup (150g) caster sugar
2 eggs
1¼ cups (185g) self-raising flour
⅓ cup (80ml) milk
pink food colouring
1 tablespoon cocoa powder
2 teaspoons milk, extra
50g milk chocolate Melts, melted
rocky road topping
½ cup (70g) unsalted roasted peanuts
1 cup (200g) red glacé cherries, halved
1 cup (100g) pink and white marshmallows, chopped coarsely
½ cup (25g) flaked coconut, toasted
200g milk eating chocolate, melted

1 Preheat oven to 180°C/160°C fan-forced. Line 6-hole texas (¾-cup/180ml) muffin pan with paper cases.
2 Beat butter, extract, sugar and eggs in small bowl with electric mixer until light and fluffy. Stir in sifted flour and milk, in two batches.
3 Divide mixture evenly among three bowls. Tint one mixture pink. Blend sifted cocoa with extra milk in cup; stir into another mixture. Leave third mixture plain.
4 Drop alternate spoonfuls of the mixtures into paper cases. Pull a skewer backwards and forwards through mixtures for a marbled effect; smooth surface.
5 Bake cakes about 30 minutes. Turn cakes onto wire rack to cool.
6 Make rocky road topping; place on top of cakes, drizzle with chocolate.
rocky road topping Combine ingredients in medium bowl.

prep + cook time 55 minutes (+ cooling) **makes** 6
tip This recipe also makes 12 standard muffins (⅓-cup/80ml capacity holes). Bake cakes for 20 minutes.

black forest cupcakes

425g can pitted cherries in syrup
165g butter, chopped coarsely
100g dark eating chocolate, chopped coarsely
1 ⅓ cups (295g) caster sugar
¼ cup (60ml) cherry brandy
1 cup (150g) plain flour
2 tablespoons self-raising flour
2 tablespoons cocoa powder
1 egg
⅔ cup (160ml) thickened cream, whipped
2 teaspoons cherry brandy, extra
100g dark eating chocolate, extra

1 Preheat oven to 160°C/140°C fan-forced. Line 6-hole texas (¾-cup/
180ml) muffin pan with paper cases.
2 Drain cherries; reserve syrup. Process ½ cup (110g) cherries with
½ cup of the syrup until smooth. Halve remaining cherries; reserve for
decorating cakes. Discard remaining syrup.
3 Stir butter, chocolate, sugar, brandy and cherry puree in small saucepan
over low heat until chocolate is melted. Transfer mixture to medium bowl;
cool 15 minutes. Whisk in sifted flours and cocoa, then egg.
4 Spoon mixture into paper cases; smooth surface. Bake cakes about
55 minutes. Turn cakes onto wire rack to cool.
5 Top cakes with remaining cherry halves and combined cream and
extra cherry brandy. Using a vegetable peeler, make small chocolate
curls from extra chocolate; sprinkle over cakes.

prep + cook time 1 hour 20 minutes (+ cooling) **makes** 6
tip This recipe also makes 12 standard muffins (⅓-cup/80ml capacity
holes). Bake cakes for 45 minutes.

chocolate ginger cupcakes

165g butter, chopped coarsely
100g dark eating chocolate,
    chopped coarsely
1⅓ cups (295g) caster sugar
⅔ cup (160ml) green ginger wine
¼ cup (60ml) water
1 cup (150g) plain flour
2 tablespoons self-raising flour
2 tablespoons cocoa powder
1 egg
⅓ cup (75g) finely chopped
    glacé ginger

chocolate decorations
100g dark chocolate Melts,
    melted
100g milk chocolate Melts,
    melted
fresh rose leaves, washed
dark chocolate ganache
200g dark eating chocolate,
    chopped coarsely
½ cup (125ml) thickened cream

1 Make chocolate decorations – gum nuts, branches and leaves.
2 Preheat oven to 160°C/140°C fan-forced. Line 6-hole texas (¾-cup/180ml) muffin pan with paper cases.
3 Stir butter, chocolate, sugar, wine and the water in small saucepan over low heat until smooth. Transfer to medium bowl; cool 15 minutes. Whisk in sifted flours and cocoa, then egg. Stir in ginger.
4 Spoon mixture into paper cases; bake cakes about 1 hour. Turn cakes onto wire rack to cool.
5 Make dark chocolate ganache; pour over cakes. Set at room temperature.
6 Decorate cakes with chocolate gum nuts, branches and leaves.
chocolate decorations For gum nuts, spread dark chocolate onto a cold surface; when set, pull a melon baller over chocolate to make gum nuts. For branches, spoon half the milk chocolate into paper piping bag; pipe branches onto a baking-paper-lined tray; leave to set. Gently lift branches off paper. For leaves, using a small, clean paint brush, paint remaining milk chocolate thickly on one side of each rose leaf, place on baking-paper-lined tray; leave to set. Carefully peel away and discard leaves.
dark chocolate ganache Place chocolate in small heatproof bowl. Bring cream to the boil in small saucepan; pour over chocolate, stir until smooth. Stand at room temperature until ganache is a thick pouring consistency.

prep + cook time 1 hour 35 minutes (+ standing & cooling) **makes** 6
tip This recipe also makes 12 standard muffins (⅓-cup/80ml capacity holes). Bake cakes for 50 minutes.

citrus cupcakes

¼ cup (40g) poppy seeds
2 tablespoons milk
125g butter, softened
1 teaspoon finely grated lemon rind
1 teaspoon finely grated lime rind
⅔ cup (150g) caster sugar
2 eggs
1 cup (150g) self-raising flour
⅓ cup (50g) plain flour
⅓ cup (40g) ground almonds
¼ cup (60ml) orange juice

450g ready-made white icing
½ cup (80g) icing sugar
green, orange and yellow food
  colouring
⅓ cup (110g) orange marmalade,
  warmed, strained
2 tablespoons each of green,
  orange and yellow sprinkles

1 Preheat oven to 180°C/160°C fan-forced. Line 6-hole texas (¾-cup/180ml) muffin pan with paper cases.
2 Combine poppy seeds and milk in small bowl; stand 20 minutes.
3 Beat butter, rinds, sugar and eggs in small bowl with electric mixer until light and fluffy. Stir in sifted flours, ground almonds, juice and poppy seed mixture.
4 Spoon mixture into paper cases; smooth surface. Bake cakes about 30 minutes. Turn cakes onto wire rack to cool.
5 Knead ready-made icing on surface dusted with sifted icing sugar until smooth; reserve 100g of icing, enclose in plastic wrap. Divide remaining icing into three equal portions; tint green, orange and yellow by kneading in colouring. Wrap separately in plastic wrap.
6 Roll each of the coloured portions to a thickness of 5mm. Cut out rounds large enough to cover tops of cakes. Brush tops of cakes with marmalade, position rounds on cakes.
7 Roll reserved icing into very thin lengths, cut off small pieces to represent seeds. Position lengths on top of cakes, using a little water, to represent segments. Fill segments with matching coloured sprinkles; position icing seeds.

prep + cook time 1 hour 10 minutes **makes** 6
tips We used green, orange and yellow paper muffin cases to match the decorations of these cakes.
This recipe also makes 12 standard muffins (⅓-cup/80ml capacity holes). Bake cakes for 20 minutes.

FRIANDS, MUFFINS & SCONES

lemon and cranberry friands

6 egg whites
185g butter, melted
1 cup (120g) ground almonds
1½ cups (240g) icing sugar
½ cup (75g) plain flour
¾ cup (105g) dried cranberries
1 tablespoon finely grated lemon rind
1 tablespoon lemon juice

1 Preheat oven to 200°C/180°C fan-forced. Grease 12-hole (½-cup/125ml) oval friand pan.
2 Whisk egg whites in medium bowl until frothy. Stir in butter, ground almonds, sifted icing sugar and flour, berries, rind and juice.
3 Spoon mixture into pan holes; bake about 20 minutes. Stand friands in pan 5 minutes; turn, top-side up, onto wire rack to cool. Serve dusted with a little sifted icing sugar.

prep + cook time 35 minutes **makes** 12

choc-hazelnut friands

6 egg whites
185g butter, melted
1 cup (100g) ground hazelnuts
1½ cups (240g) icing sugar
½ cup (75g) plain flour
1 tablespoon cocoa powder
100g dark eating chocolate, chopped finely
¼ cup (35g) coarsely chopped, roasted hazelnuts

1 Preheat oven to 200°C/180°C fan-forced. Line 12-hole (½-cup/125ml) oval friand pan with paper cases.
2 Whisk egg whites in medium bowl until frothy. Stir in butter, ground hazelnuts, sifted icing sugar, flour and cocoa, and chocolate. Spoon mixture into pan holes; sprinkle with nuts.
3 Bake friands about 25 minutes. Stand friands in pan 5 minutes; turn, top-side up, onto wire rack to cool.

prep + cook time 50 minutes **makes** 12

lemon curd friands

6 egg whites
185g butter, melted
1 cup (120g) ground almonds
1½ cups (240g) icing sugar
½ cup (75g) plain flour
¼ cup (80g) lemon curd

1 Preheat oven to 200°C/180°C fan-forced. Grease 12-hole (½-cup/ 125ml) oval friand pan.
2 Whisk egg whites in medium bowl until frothy. Stir in butter, ground almonds, sifted icing sugar and flour.
3 Spoon mixture into pan holes; bake 10 minutes.
4 Remove friands from oven; top each with a level teaspoon of curd. Bake a further 10 minutes. Stand friands in pan 5 minutes; turn, top-side up, onto wire rack to cool.

prep + cook time 35 minutes **makes** 12

fruit mince friands

6 egg whites
185g unsalted butter, melted
1 teaspoon finely grated orange rind
1 cup (120g) ground almonds
1½ cups (240g) icing sugar
½ cup (75g) plain flour
½ cup (150g) fruit mince

1 Preheat oven to 180°C/160°C fan-forced. Grease 12-hole (½-cup/125ml) oval friand pan.
2 Whisk egg whites in medium bowl until frothy. Stir in butter, rind, ground almonds, then sifted icing sugar and flour.
3 Spoon mixture into pan holes; bake 10 minutes.
4 Remove friands from oven; press a small, 1cm-deep hole in top of each friand with the end of a wooden spoon. Spoon fruit mince into holes; bake a further 10 minutes. Stand friands in pan 5 minutes; turn, top-side up, onto wire rack to cool. Serve dusted with sifted icing sugar.

prep + cook time 35 minutes **makes** 12

coffee and walnut friands

1¼ cups (125g) roasted walnuts
2 teaspoons instant coffee granules
2 teaspoons boiling water
6 egg whites
185g butter, melted
1½ cups (240g) icing sugar
½ cup (75g) plain flour
24 whole coffee beans

1 Preheat oven to 200°C/180°C fan-forced. Grease 12-hole (½-cup/ 125ml) oval friand pan.
2 Process nuts until ground finely.
3 Stir coffee and the water in small jug until dissolved.
4 Whisk egg whites in medium bowl until frothy. Stir in butter, sifted icing sugar and flour, nuts and coffee mixture. Spoon mixture into pan holes; top each with two coffee beans.
5 Bake friands about 20 minutes. Stand friands in pan 5 minutes; turn, top-side up, onto wire rack to cool. Serve dusted with a little sifted icing sugar.

prep + cook time 35 minutes **makes** 12

mandarin and poppy seed friands

2 large mandarins (500g)
1 tablespoon poppy seeds
6 egg whites
185g butter, melted
1 cup (120g) ground almonds
1½ cups (240g) icing sugar
½ cup (75g) plain flour

1 Preheat oven to 200°C/180°C fan-forced. Line 12-hole (½-cup/125ml) oval friand pan with paper cases.
2 Finely grate rind from mandarins (you need 2 tablespoons of rind); juice the mandarins (you need 2 tablespoons of juice).
3 Combine poppy seeds and juice in small jug; stand 10 minutes.
4 Whisk egg whites in medium bowl until frothy. Stir in butter, ground almonds, sifted icing sugar and flour, rind and poppy seed mixture.
5 Spoon mixture into pan holes; bake about 20 minutes. Stand friands in pan 5 minutes; turn, top-side up, onto wire rack to cool. Serve dusted with a little sifted icing sugar.

prep + cook time 35 minutes **makes** 12

brandied cherry friands

1 cup (150g) frozen seeded cherries
2 tablespoons brandy
1 cup (120g) roasted pecans
6 egg whites
185g butter, melted
1½ cups (240g) icing sugar
½ cup (75g) plain flour
cherry sauce
¼ cup (55g) caster sugar
2 tablespoons water

1 Preheat oven to 200°C/180°C fan-forced. Grease 12-hole (½-cup/ 125ml) oval friand pan.
2 Combine cherries and brandy in small bowl; stand 30 minutes. Drain cherries; reserve liquid.
3 Process nuts until ground finely.
4 Whisk egg whites in medium bowl until frothy. Stir in butter, sifted icing sugar and flour, and nuts. Spoon mixture into pan holes; top with drained cherries.
5 Bake friands about 20 minutes. Stand friands in pan 5 minutes; turn, top-side up, onto serving plates.
6 Meanwhile, make cherry sauce. Serve friands with sauce.
cherry sauce Stir sugar, the water and reserved cherry juice in small saucepan over low heat until sugar dissolves. Bring to the boil; reduce heat. Simmer, uncovered, about 3 minutes or until sauce thickens slightly.

prep + cook time 35 minutes (+ standing) **makes** 12

coconut and pineapple friands

6 egg whites
185g butter, melted
1 cup (120g) ground almonds
1 ½ cups (240g) icing sugar
⅓ cup (50g) plain flour
¾ cup (170g) finely chopped glacé pineapple
½ cup (40g) shredded coconut

1 Preheat oven to 200°C/180°C fan-forced. Line 12-hole (½-cup/125ml) oval friand pan with paper cases.
2 Whisk egg whites in medium bowl until frothy. Stir in butter, ground almonds, sifted icing sugar and flour, pineapple and ⅓ cup of the coconut. Spoon mixture into pan holes; sprinkle with remaining coconut.
3 Bake friands about 20 minutes. Stand friands in pan 5 minutes; turn, top-side up, onto wire rack to cool.

prep + cook time 35 minutes **makes** 12

pistachio and lime friands

1 cup (140g) unsalted roasted pistachios
6 egg whites
185g butter, melted
1½ cups (240g) icing sugar
½ cup (75g) plain flour
2 teaspoons finely grated lime rind
1 tablespoon lime juice

1 Preheat oven to 200°C/180°C fan-forced. Line 12-hole (½-cup/ 125ml) oval friand pan.
2 Process nuts until ground finely.
3 Whisk egg whites in medium bowl until frothy. Stir in butter, sifted icing sugar and flour, rind, juice and ground pistachios.
4 Spoon mixture into pan holes; bake about 25 minutes. Stand friands in pan 5 minutes; turn, top-side up, onto wire rack to cool. Serve dusted with a little sifted icing sugar.

prep + cook time 50 minutes **makes** 12

christmas muffins

2½ cups (450g) self-raising flour
100g butter, chopped
1 cup (220g) caster sugar
1¼ cups (310ml) buttermilk
1 egg, beaten lightly
1 cup (250g) mixed coarsely chopped glacé fruit
250g ready-made white icing
2 tablespoons apricot jam, warmed, strained

1 Preheat oven to 200°C/180°C fan-forced. Grease 12-hole (⅓-cup/80ml) muffin pan.
2 Sift flour into medium bowl; rub in butter. Gently stir in sugar, buttermilk and egg. Gently stir in 1 cup mixed coarsely chopped glacé fruit.
3 Spoon mixture into pan holes; bake about 20 minutes. Stand muffins in pan 5 minutes; turn, top-side up, onto wire rack to cool.
4 Roll icing out to 5mm thick; cut out 12 x 4.5cm stars. Brush tops of muffins with jam; top with icing stars. Dust with a little sifted icing sugar, if you like.

prep + cook time 40 minutes **makes** 12

date muffins with orange syrup

1 ¼ cups (185g) white self-raising flour
1 cup (160g) wholemeal self-raising flour
1 cup (220g) caster sugar
100g butter, melted
1 cup (280g) yogurt
2 eggs
1 teaspoon finely grated orange rind
1 ½ cups (210g) coarsely chopped seeded dried dates
orange syrup
½ cup (110g) caster sugar
¼ cup (60ml) water
2 teaspoons finely grated orange rind
¼ cup (60ml) orange juice

1 Preheat oven to 200°C/180°C fan-forced. Grease 12-hole (⅓-cup/80ml) muffin pan with butter.
2 Sift flours and sugar into large bowl. Stir in combined butter, yogurt, eggs and rind. Do not overmix; mixture should be lumpy. Stir in dates.
3 Spoon mixture into pan holes; bake about 20 minutes.
4 Meanwhile, make orange syrup.
5 Stand muffins in pan 2 minutes; turn, top-side up, onto wire rack. Stand rack over tray. Pierce muffins all over with skewer; pour hot syrup over hot muffins.
orange syrup Stir ingredients in small saucepan over heat until sugar dissolves. Bring to the boil. Reduce heat; simmer, uncovered, 2 minutes.

prep + cook time 35 minutes **makes** 12

banana, cranberry and macadamia muffins

You need about 2 medium overripe bananas (400g) to get the required amount of mashed banana.

2¼ cups (335g) self-raising flour
¾ cup (165g) caster sugar
½ cup (65g) dried cranberries
½ cup (70g) coarsely chopped roasted unsalted macadamias
⅔ cup mashed banana
2 eggs, beaten lightly
1 cup (250ml) milk
½ cup (125ml) vegetable oil

1 Preheat oven to 200°C/180°C fan-forced. Line three six-hole (⅓-cup/80ml) muffin pans with paper cases.
2 Sift flour and sugar into large bowl; stir in berries and nuts. Stir in combined remaining ingredients; do not overmix, mixture should be lumpy.
3 Spoon mixture into pan holes; bake about 20 minutes. Stand muffins 5 minutes; turn, top-side up, onto wire rack to cool. Serve dusted with sifted icing sugar.

prep + cook time 30 minutes **makes** 18

warm malt truffle muffins

60g unsalted butter
⅓ cup (125g) barley malt syrup
1¼ cups (185g) self-raising flour
¼ cup (30g) malted milk powder
2 tablespoons cocoa powder
pinch bicarbonate of soda
¼ cup (55g) brown sugar
½ cup (125ml) milk
1 egg
¾ cup (180ml) cream

malt truffles
200g milk eating chocolate,
　chopped coarsely
¼ cup (60ml) cream
½ cup (60g) malted milk powder

1 Make malt truffles.
2 Preheat oven to 180°C/160°C fan-forced. Line 12-hole (⅓-cup/80ml) muffin pan with paper cases.
3 Stir butter and malt syrup in small saucepan over low heat until smooth.
4 Sift flour, malt powder, cocoa, soda and sugar into medium bowl. Stir in butter mixture, milk and egg. Do not overmix; mixture should be lumpy.
5 Spoon half the mixture into cases. Place a truffle into each case; top with remaining mixture. Bake about 20 minutes; cool 2 minutes, then remove paper cases.
6 Meanwhile, stir reserved malt truffle mixture and cream in small saucepan, over low heat, until malt sauce is smooth.
7 Serve warm muffins with warm sauce. Dust with sifted cocoa powder, if you like.
malt truffles Stir ingredients in small heatproof bowl over small saucepan of simmering water until smooth. Reserve ½ cup (125ml) mixture for malt sauce. Refrigerate remaining mixture about 30 minutes or until firm. Roll heaped teaspoons of refrigerated mixture into balls; place on baking-paper-lined tray. Freeze until firm.

prep + cook time 1 hour (+ refrigeration & freezing) **makes** 12

apple streusel muffins

40g butter
3 large apples (600g), peeled,
   cut into 1cm pieces
⅓ cup (75g) firmly packed
   brown sugar
2 cups (300g) self-raising flour
1 teaspoon mixed spice
⅔ cup (150g) caster sugar
80g butter, melted, extra
¾ cup (180ml) buttermilk
1 egg

streusel topping
⅓ cup (50g) self-raising flour
⅓ cup (50g) plain flour
⅓ cup (75g) firmly packed
   brown sugar
½ teaspoon ground cinnamon
80g cold butter, chopped coarsely

1 Make streusel topping.
2 Meanwhile, melt butter in large frying pan; cook apple, stirring,
about 5 minutes or until browned lightly. Add brown sugar; cook,
stirring, about 5 minutes or until mixture thickens. Cool.
3 Preheat oven to 200°C/180°C fan-forced. Line 12-hole (⅓-cup/
80ml) muffin pan with paper cases.
4 Sift flour, spice and sugar into large bowl. Stir in combined extra
butter, buttermilk and egg. Do not overmix; mixture should be lumpy.
Stir in half the apple mixture.
5 Spoon mixture into pan holes; top with remaining apple mixture.
Coarsely grate streusel topping over muffin mixture.
6 Bake muffins about 20 minutes. Stand muffins in pan 5 minutes;
turn, top-side up, onto wire rack to cool.
streusel topping Process flours, sugar and cinnamon until combined.
Add butter; process until combined. Roll dough into ball, wrap in plastic
wrap; freeze about 15 minutes or until firm.

prep + cook time 40 minutes (+ freezing) **makes** 12

choc-chip jaffa muffins

2½ cups (375g) self-raising flour
100g cold butter, chopped finely
1 cup (220g) caster sugar
1¼ cups (310ml) buttermilk
1 egg
¾ cup (135g) dark Choc Bits
2 teaspoons finely grated orange rind

1 Preheat oven to 200°C/180°C fan-forced. Grease 12-hole (⅓-cup/ 80ml) muffin pan.
2 Sift flour into large bowl; rub in butter. Stir in sugar, buttermilk and egg. Do not overmix; mixture should be lumpy. Stir in Choc Bits and rind.
3 Spoon mixture into pan holes; bake about 20 minutes. Stand muffins in pan 5 minutes; turn, top-side up, onto wire rack to cool.

prep + cook time 30 minutes **makes** 12

triple choc muffins

1¾ cups (260g) self-raising flour
½ cup (50g) cocoa powder
¾ cup (165g) firmly packed brown sugar
½ cup (95g) dark Choc Bits
½ cup (95g) white Choc Bits
2 eggs
1 cup (250ml) buttermilk
⅔ cup (160ml) vegetable oil
12 white chocolate Melts

1 Preheat oven to 200°C/180°C fan-forced. Line 12-hole (⅓-cup/80ml) muffin pan with paper cases.
2 Sift flour and cocoa into large bowl; stir in sugar and Choc Bits. Stir in combined eggs, buttermilk and oil. Do not overmix; mixture should be lumpy.
3 Spoon mixture into paper cases; bake 20 minutes. Remove from oven; top each muffin with a chocolate Melt. Bake a further 2 minutes. Stand muffins in pan 5 minutes; turn, top-side up, onto wire rack to cool.

prep + cook time 35 minutes **makes** 12

ginger and pear muffins

2 cups (300g) self-raising flour
1 teaspoon ground ginger
¾ cup (165g) caster sugar
80g butter, melted
1 cup (280g) yogurt
2 eggs
2 medium pears (460g), peeled, chopped finely
muesli topping
50g butter
2 tablespoons honey
2 cups (220g) natural muesli

1 Preheat oven to 200°C/180°C fan-forced. Line 12-hole (⅓-cup/80ml) muffin pan with paper cases.
2 Make muesli topping.
3 Sift flour and ginger into large bowl; stir in sugar and combined butter, yogurt and eggs. Do not overmix; mixture should be lumpy. Gently stir in pears.
4 Spoon mixture into pan holes; spoon muesli topping onto muffin mixture. Bake about 20 minutes. Stand muffins in pan 5 minutes; turn, top-side up, onto wire rack to cool.
muesli topping Stir butter and honey in small saucepan over low heat until combined. Remove from heat; stir in muesli.

prep + cook time 35 minutes **makes** 12

butterscotch pecan muffins

¾ cup (240g) top 'n' fill caramel
2 cups (300g) self-raising flour
¾ cup (165g) firmly packed brown sugar
¾ cup (90g) coarsely chopped roasted pecans
80g butter, melted
1 cup (250ml) buttermilk
1 egg

1 Preheat oven to 200°C/180°C fan-forced. Line 12-hole (⅓-cup/80ml) muffin pan with paper cases.
2 Stir caramel in small saucepan over low heat until smooth. Cool 5 minutes.
3 Meanwhile, sift flour and sugar into large bowl. Stir in nuts and combined butter, buttermilk and egg. Do not overmix; mixture should be lumpy.
4 Spoon half the mixture into paper cases, spoon half the caramel over muffin mixture; top with remaining mixture then caramel. Using a skewer, gently swirl caramel into muffin mixture.
5 Bake muffins about 20 minutes. Stand muffins in pan 5 minutes; turn, top-side up, onto wire rack to cool.

prep + cook time 40 minutes **makes** 12

chocolate raspberry dessert muffins

1¾ cups (260g) self-raising flour
¼ cup (25g) cocoa powder
¾ cup (165g) caster sugar
50g butter, melted
⅔ cup (160ml) milk
½ cup (120g) sour cream
2 eggs
½ cup (70g) coarsely chopped roasted hazelnuts
150g dark eating chocolate, chopped coarsely
1 cup (150g) frozen raspberries

1 Preheat oven to 200°C/180°C fan-forced. Line 12-hole (⅓-cup/80ml) muffin pan with paper cases.
2 Sift flour, cocoa and sugar into large bowl. Stir in combined butter, milk, sour cream and eggs. Do not overmix; mixture should be lumpy. Stir in remaining ingredients.
3 Spoon mixture into cases; bake about 20 minutes. Stand muffins in pan 5 minutes; turn, top-side up, onto wire rack to cool.

prep + cook time 35 minutes **makes** 12

rhubarb and custard muffins

2 cups (300g) self-raising flour
½ cup (75g) plain flour
¾ cup (165g) caster sugar
100g butter, melted
1 cup (250ml) milk
1 egg
3 cups (330g) finely chopped rhubarb
1 tablespoon demerara sugar
custard
2 tablespoons custard powder
¼ cup (55g) caster sugar
1 cup (250ml) milk
1 teaspoon vanilla extract

1 Make custard.
2 Preheat oven to 200°C/180°C fan-forced. Line 12-hole (⅓-cup/80ml) muffin pan with paper cases.
3 Sift flours and caster sugar into large bowl. Stir in combined butter, milk and egg. Do not overmix; mixture should be lumpy. Stir in half the rhubarb.
4 Spoon half the mixture among paper cases; top with custard. Spoon remaining mixture over custard. Sprinkle with remaining rhubarb and demerara sugar.
5 Bake muffins about 25 minutes. Stand muffins in pan 5 minutes; turn, top-side up, onto wire rack to cool. Serve dusted with a little sifted icing sugar.
custard Combine custard powder and sugar in small saucepan; gradually stir in milk. Stir mixture over medium heat until custard boils and thickens. Stir in extract; cool.

prep + cook time 50 minutes **makes** 12

berry buttermilk muffins

2½ cups (375g) self-raising flour
100g butter, chopped coarsely
1 cup (220g) caster sugar
1¼ cups (310ml) buttermilk
1 egg, beaten lightly
1⅓ cups (200g) frozen mixed berries

1 Preheat oven to 200°C/180°C fan-forced. Line 12-hole (⅓-cup/80ml) muffin pan with paper cases.
2 Sift flour into large bowl; rub in butter using fingers. Stir in sugar, buttermilk and egg. Do not overmix; mixture should be lumpy. Stir in berries.
3 Spoon mixture into pan holes; bake about 20 minutes. Stand muffins in pan 5 minutes; turn, top-side up, onto wire rack to cool.

prep + cook time 30 minutes **makes** 12

basic scones

2½ cups (375g) self-raising flour
1 tablespoon caster sugar
¼ teaspoon salt
30g butter
¾ cup (180ml) milk
½ cup (125ml) water, approximately

1 Preheat oven to 220°C/200°C fan-forced. Grease deep 19cm-square cake pan.
2 Sift flour, sugar and salt into large bowl; rub in butter with fingertips. Make well in centre of mixture; add milk and almost all of the water. Using a knife, cut the milk and the water through the flour mixture to mix to a soft, sticky dough. Add remaining water only if needed. Knead dough on floured surface until smooth.
3 Press dough out evenly to 2cm thickness. Cut as many 4.5cm rounds as you can from dough. Place rounds side by side, just touching, in pan. Gently knead scraps of dough together; repeat pressing and cutting of dough, place in same pan. Brush tops with a little extra milk.
4 Bake scones about 15 minutes or until browned and scones sound hollow when tapped firmly on the top with fingers.

variation
date scones When making the basic scone mixture, stir ¾ cup (120g) finely chopped seeded dried dates into the flour mixture after the butter has been rubbed in. Also, replace the milk and water with 1¼ cups (310ml) buttermilk.

prep + cook time 45 minutes **makes** 16

pumpkin scones

40g butter
¼ cup (55g) caster sugar
1 egg, beaten lightly
¾ cup cooked mashed pumpkin
2½ cups (375g) self-raising flour
½ teaspoon ground nutmeg
⅓ cup (180ml) milk, approximately

1 Preheat oven to 220°C/200°C fan-forced. Grease two 20cm-round sandwich pans.
2 Beat butter and sugar in small bowl with electric mixer until light and fluffy; beat in egg. Transfer mixture to large bowl; stir in pumpkin, then sifted dry ingredients and enough milk to make a soft sticky dough. Knead dough on floured surface until smooth.
3 Press dough out evenly to 2cm thickness. Cut as many 5cm rounds as you can from dough. Place rounds side by side, just touching, in pans. Gently knead scraps of dough together; repeat pressing and cutting of dough, place in same pan. Brush tops with a little extra milk.
4 Bake scones about 15 minutes or until browned and scones sound hollow when tapped firmly on the top with fingers.

prep + cook time 35 minutes **makes** 16

plum jam scone ring

2 cups (300g) self-raising flour
1 tablespoon caster sugar
30g butter, chopped coarsely
¾ cup (180ml) milk
1 egg yolk
¼ cup (80g) plum jam
½ cup (80g) coarsely chopped raisins
1 tablespoon icing sugar

1 Preheat oven to 200°C/180°C fan-forced. Grease oven tray; line with baking paper.
2 Sift flour and sugar into medium bowl; rub in butter. Add combined milk and egg yolk; using a knife, cut milk mixture through flour mixture to make a soft, sticky dough. Knead dough on floured surface until smooth. Roll dough into 30cm x 40cm rectangle.
3 Spread jam over dough; sprinkle with raisins. Roll dough firmly (but not too tightly) from one long side; place log on tray. Curve log to form a ring; press ends together to seal. Cut around outside of ring at 4cm intervals, cutting all the way down to the tray but not cutting all the way through to the inside of the ring.
4 Bake about 30 minutes. Serve warm dusted with sifted icing sugar.

prep + cook time 45 minutes **serves** 8

spiced apple scones

3½ cups (525g) self-raising flour
2 tablespoons icing sugar
1 teaspoon ground nutmeg
1 teaspoon ground cinnamon
60g cold butter, chopped coarsely
⅔ cup (160ml) water
1½ cups (375ml) buttermilk
1 cup (75g) finely chopped dried apple
1 tablespoon milk
golden syrup butter
100g butter, softened
1 tablespoon golden syrup

1 Preheat oven to 220°C/200°C fan-forced. Grease deep 22cm x 32cm rectangular cake pan.
2 Sift flour, icing sugar and spices into large bowl; rub in butter. Add the water, buttermilk and apple to flour mixture. Using a knife, cut buttermilk through the mixture to make a soft, sticky dough. Knead dough on floured surface until smooth.
3 Press dough out evenly to 2cm thickness. Cut as many 5cm rounds as you can from dough. Place rounds side by side, just touching, in pan. Gently knead scraps of dough together; repeat pressing and cutting of dough, place in pan. Brush tops with a little milk.
4 Bake scones about 15 minutes.
5 Meanwhile, make golden syrup butter. Serve hot scones with golden syrup butter.
golden syrup butter Whisk ingredients in medium bowl until light and fluffy.

prep + cook time 30 minutes **makes** 20

DESSERT CAKES

rich mocha gâteau

½ cup (125ml) Cointreau
2 teaspoons grated orange rind
150g milk chocolate, melted
90g unsalted butter, melted
6 eggs, separated
¾ cup (110g) self-raising flour
⅓ cup (75g) caster sugar
rich mocha filling
2 teaspoons instant coffee granules
2 tablespoons hot water
300g dark eating chocolate, melted
6 egg yolks

chocolate butter cream
2 tablespoons instant coffee
granules
¼ cup (60ml) hot water
200g dark eating chocolate,
melted
4 egg yolks
¼ cup (55g) caster sugar
185g unsalted butter, softened

1 Preheat oven to 180°C/160°C fan-forced. Grease deep 22cm-round cake pan; line base with baking paper.
2 Stand liqueur and rind in small bowl 30 minutes. Strain; reserve rind and liqueur separately.
3 Combine chocolate, butter and rind in large bowl. Stir in 3 teaspoons of the liqueur, egg yolks and sifted flour.
4 Beat egg whites in large bowl with electric mixer until soft peaks form; gradually add sugar, beating until dissolved between additions. Fold whites into chocolate mixture, in two batches.
5 Pour mixture into pan; bake about 35 minutes. Stand cake in pan 5 minutes; turn, top-side up, onto wire rack to cool.
6 Meanwhile, make rich mocha filling and chocolate butter cream.
7 Split cake into three layers. Place first layer on serving plate; spread with half the mocha filling. Refrigerate 15 minutes. Top with second layer; spread with remaining mocha filling. Top with third layer; refrigerate 30 minutes. Spread butter cream all over cake; refrigerate 30 minutes.
rich mocha filling Combine coffee and the water in large bowl; stir in chocolate, then yolks and ⅓ cup of remaining liqueur. Refrigerate until set.
chocolate butter cream Combine coffee and the water in large bowl; stir in chocolate and remaining liqueur. Beat yolks and sugar in small bowl with electric mixer until thick and creamy; beat in butter in several batches until smooth. Gradually beat in chocolate mixture; refrigerate 10 minutes or until spreadable.

prep + cook time 1 hour 10 minutes (+ refrigeration) **serves** 12

dark chocolate and almond torte

160g dark eating chocolate, chopped coarsely
160g unsalted butter
5 eggs, separated
¾ cup (165g) caster sugar
1 cup (120g) ground almonds
⅔ cup (50g) roasted flaked almonds, chopped coarsely
⅓ cup (35g) coarsely grated dark eating chocolate
1 cup (140g) vienna almonds
dark chocolate ganache
125g dark eating chocolate, chopped coarsely
⅓ cup (80ml) cream

1 Preheat oven to 180°C/160°C fan-forced. Grease deep 22cm-round cake pan; line base and side with baking paper.
2 Stir chopped chocolate and butter in small saucepan over low heat until smooth; cool.
3 Beat egg yolks and sugar in small bowl with electric mixer until thick and creamy. Transfer to large bowl; stir in chocolate mixture, ground almonds, flaked almonds and grated chocolate.
4 Beat egg whites in small bowl with electric mixer until soft peaks form; fold into chocolate mixture, in two batches.
5 Pour mixture into pan; bake about 45 minutes. Stand cake in pan 15 minutes; turn, top-side up, onto wire rack to cool.
6 Make dark chocolate ganache; spread over cake. Decorate cake with vienna almonds; stand 30 minutes before serving.
dark chocolate ganache Stir ingredients in small saucepan over low heat until smooth.

prep + cook time 1 hour 15 minutes (+ standing) **serves** 12

banana caramel layer cake

You need about 2 large overripe bananas (460g) to get the required amount of mashed banana.

185g butter, softened
1¼ cup (175g) caster sugar
3 eggs
2¼ cups (335g) self-raising flour
½ teaspoon bicarbonate of soda
1¼ cups mashed banana
⅓ cup (80ml) milk
380g can top 'n' fill caramel
¾ cup (180ml) thickened cream, whipped
1 large banana (230g), extra, sliced thinly

1 Preheat oven to 180°C/160°C fan-forced. Grease 24cm bundt pan or 24cm patterned silicone pan well.
2 Beat butter and sugar in small bowl with electric mixer until light and fluffy. Beat in eggs, one at a time. Transfer mixture to large bowl; stir in sifted dry ingredients, mashed banana and milk.
3 Spread mixture into pan; bake about 40 minutes. Stand cake in pan 5 minutes; turn onto wire rack to cool.
4 Split cake into three layers. Spread bottom layer of cake with half the caramel, top with half the cream then half the banana slices. Repeat next layer using remaining caramel, cream and banana slices. Replace top of cake. Dust with icing sugar before serving.

prep + cook time 1 hour (+ cooling) **serves** 12

flourless chocolate dessert cake

100g dark eating chocolate, chopped
100g butter, chopped
½ cup (110g) caster sugar
2 tablespoons marsala
⅔ cup (80g) ground almonds
1 tablespoon instant coffee granules
1 tablespoon hot water
3 eggs, separated
strawberry coulis
250g strawberries
¼ cup (40g) icing sugar

1 Preheat oven to 180°C/160°C fan-forced. Grease deep 20cm-round cake pan; line base and side with baking paper.
2 Melt chocolate and butter in small saucepan, over low heat, stirring, until mixture is combined.
3 Combine chocolate mixture with sugar, marsala, ground almonds and combined coffee and the water in a large bowl; beat in egg yolks, one at a time.
4 Beat egg whites in small bowl with electric mixer until soft peaks form; gently fold into chocolate mixture, in two batches.
5 Pour mixture into pan; bake about 45 minutes. Cool cake in pan, cover; refrigerate several hours or overnight.
6 Make strawberry coulis.
7 Carefully turn cake onto board; cut into slices with a hot knife. Serve cake with strawberry coulis. Dust with sifted icing sugar and serve with whipped cream, if you like.
strawberry coulis Blend or process ingredients until mixture is smooth.

prep + cook time 1 hour (+ refrigeration) **serves** 6

black forest cake

250g butter, chopped
1 tablespoon instant coffee granules
1½ cups (375ml) hot water
200g dark eating chocolate, chopped
2 cups (440g) caster sugar
1½ cups (225g) self-raising flour
1 cup (150g) plain flour
¼ cup (25g) cocoa powder
2 eggs
2 teaspoons vanilla extract
¼ cup (60ml) kirsch
600ml thickened cream, whipped
2 x 425g cans seeded black cherries, drained, halved
2 teaspoons cocoa powder, extra

1 Preheat oven to 150°C/130°C fan-forced. Grease deep 22cm-round cake pan; line base and side with baking paper.
2 Melt butter in medium saucepan; stir in combined coffee and hot water, then chocolate and sugar. Stir over low heat, without boiling, until smooth. Transfer mixture to large bowl; cool to warm.
3 Beat chocolate mixture on low speed with electric mixer; gradually beat in sifted dry ingredients, in three batches. Beat in eggs, one at a time, then extract.
4 Pour mixture into pan; bake about 1¾ hours. Stand cake in pan 5 minutes; turn, top-side up, onto wire rack to cool.
5 Trim top of cake to make it flat. Split cake into three even layers. Place one layer onto serving plate; brush with half of the kirsch, top with half of the cream and half of the cherries. Repeat layering, then top with cake top. Dust with extra sifted cocoa.

prep + cook time 2 hours 25 minutes (+ cooling) **serves** 12
tip Kirsch is a cherry-flavoured liqueur.

soft-centred mocha cakes

150g dark eating chocolate, chopped coarsely
125g butter, chopped coarsely
3 teaspoons instant coffee granules
2 eggs
2 egg yolks
⅓ cup (75g) caster sugar
¼ cup (35g) plain flour
2 teaspoons cocoa powder

1 Preheat oven to 200°C/180°C fan-forced. Grease six-hole (¾-cup/180ml) texas muffin pan well with softened butter.
2 Stir chocolate, butter and coffee in small saucepan, over low heat, until smooth; cool 10 minutes. Transfer mixture to large bowl.
3 Beat eggs, egg yolks and sugar in small bowl with electric mixer until thick and creamy. Fold egg mixture and sifted flour into barely warm chocolate mixture.
4 Spoon mixture among pan holes; bake 12 minutes.
5 Gently turn puddings onto serving plates, top-side down. Serve immediately, dusted with sifted cocoa powder; top with fresh raspberries and whipped cream, if you like.

prep + cook time 45 minutes **makes** 6
tip Use a good quality dark chocolate with 70% cocoa solids.

flourless fig, pecan and maple syrup cake

You need to blend 2 cups (240g) pecans to get the required amount
  of ground pecans.

125g butter, softened
½ cup (110g) firmly packed brown sugar
4 eggs, separated
1½ cups (180g) ground pecans
⅓ cup (55g) semolina
¼ cup (60ml) milk
1 cup (200g) finely chopped dried figs
maple syrup
½ cup (125ml) maple syrup
⅓ cup (75g) firmly packed brown sugar
½ cup (125ml) water

1 Preheat oven to 180°C/160°C fan-forced. Grease deep 23cm-round cake pan; line base and side with baking paper.
2 Beat butter and sugar in small bowl with electric mixer until light and fluffy. Beat in egg yolks. Transfer mixture to large bowl; stir in ground pecans and semolina, then milk and figs.
3 Beat egg whites in small bowl with electric mixer until soft peaks form; fold into fig mixture, in two batches.
4 Pour mixture into pan; bake about 40 minutes. Stand cake in pan 5 minutes; turn, top-side up, onto wire rack set over tray.
5 Meanwhile, make maple syrup. Pour hot syrup over hot cake. Serve cake warm.
maple syrup Stir ingredients in small saucepan over low heat until sugar dissolves; bring to the boil. Boil, uncovered, about 5 minutes or until thickened slightly.

prep + cook time 1 hour **serves** 12

vanilla pear almond cake

8 corella pears (800g)
2½ cups (625ml) water
1 strip lemon rind
1¾ cups (385g) caster sugar
1 vanilla bean
125g butter, softened
3 eggs
⅔ cup (160g) sour cream
⅔ cup (100g) plain flour
⅔ cup (100g) self-raising flour
¼ cup (40g) blanched almonds, roasted, chopped coarsely
40g dark eating chocolate, chopped coarsely
½ cup (60g) ground almonds

1 Peel pears, leaving stems intact.
2 Combine the water, rind and 1 cup of the sugar in medium saucepan.
Split vanilla bean in half lengthways; scrape seeds into pan, then add
pod. Stir over heat, without boiling, until sugar dissolves. Add pears; bring
to the boil. Reduce heat; simmer, covered, 30 minutes or until pears are
just tender. Transfer pears to medium bowl; bring syrup to the boil. Boil,
uncovered, until syrup reduces by half. Cool completely.
3 Preheat oven to 160°C/140°C fan-forced. Insert base of 23cm
springform tin upside down in tin to give a flat base; grease tin.
4 Beat butter and remaining sugar in medium bowl with electric mixer
until light and fluffy. Beat in eggs, one at a time; beat in sour cream.
Stir in 2 tablespoons of the syrup, then sifted flours, almonds, chocolate
and ground almonds.
5 Spread mixture into tin; place pears upright around edge of tin, gently
pushing to the bottom.
6 Bake cake about 1 hour 35 minutes. Stand cake in pan 10 minutes;
remove from tin. Serve cake warm, brushed with remaining syrup.

prep + cook time 2 hours 45 minutes (+ cooling) **serves** 8

tiramisu cakes

460g double unfilled round sponge cake
2 tablespoons instant coffee granules
¼ cup (60ml) boiling water
⅓ cup (80ml) coffee-flavoured liqueur
1 teaspoon gelatine
1 tablespoon boiling water, extra
¾ cup (180ml) thickened cream
¼ cup (40g) icing sugar
1 teaspoon vanilla extract
1½ cups (375g) mascarpone cheese
ganache
180g dark eating chocolate, chopped coarsely
⅔ cup (160ml) cream

1 Make ganache.
2 Line each hole of a greased six-hole (¾-cup/180ml) texas muffin pan with plastic wrap. Divide half the ganache over the base of each pan hole. Refrigerate 20 minutes.
3 Meanwhile, cut each sponge cake into three slices horizontally. Cut six 8cm rounds from three sponge slices and six 7cm rounds from remaining three sponge slices.
4 Dissolve coffee in the boiling water in small jug; stir in liqueur. Sprinkle gelatine over the extra boiling water in another small jug; stir until gelatine dissolves. Cool.
5 Beat cream, sifted icing sugar and extract in small bowl with electric mixer until soft peaks form; beat in gelatine mixture. Transfer mixture to large bowl; fold in cheese.
6 Brush both sides of sponge rounds with coffee mixture. Spread half the cheese mixture into pan holes; top with small sponge rounds. Spread remaining cheese mixture over sponge layers; top with larger sponge rounds, spread with remaining ganache. Refrigerate 3 hours or overnight.
7 Remove tiramisu from pan; turn, top-side down, onto serving plates, remove plastic wrap. Serve dusted with a little sifted cocoa powder.
ganache Place chocolate in small bowl. Bring cream to the boil in small saucepan; remove from heat. Add chocolate; stir until smooth.

prep + cook time 40 minutes (+ refrigeration) **makes** 6

flourless chocolate cakes with latte sauce

150g dark eating chocolate, chopped coarsely
150g butter, chopped coarsely
4 eggs, separated
1 cup (220g) firmly packed brown sugar
1¼ cups (150g) ground almonds
latte sauce
180g white eating chocolate, chopped coarsely
½ cup (125ml) cream
2 tablespoons coffee-flavoured liqueur
1 teaspoon instant coffee granules

1 Preheat oven to 180°C/160°C fan-forced. Grease 12-hole (⅓-cup/ 80ml) muffin pan.
2 Make latte sauce.
3 Stir chocolate and butter in medium saucepan over low heat until smooth. Cool 5 minutes. Stir in egg yolks, sugar and ground almonds. Transfer mixture to large bowl.
4 Beat egg whites in small bowl with electric mixer until soft peaks form; fold into chocolate mixture, in two batches.
5 Spoon mixture into pan holes; bake about 25 minutes. Cool cakes in pan 5 minutes before turning, top-side down, onto serving plates. Serve warm cakes drizzled with latte sauce.
latte sauce Stir ingredients in small saucepan over low heat until smooth. Cool about 30 minutes or until thickened slightly.

prep + cook time 45 minutes (+ cooling) **makes** 12

rich truffle mud cake

6 eggs
½ cup (110g) firmly packed brown sugar
400g dark eating chocolate, melted
1 cup (250ml) thick cream (48% fat content)
⅓ cup (80ml) orange-flavoured liqueur

1 Preheat oven to 180°C/160°C fan-forced. Grease deep 22cm-round cake pan; line base and side with baking paper.
2 Beat eggs and sugar in large bowl with electric mixer until thick and creamy. With motor operating, gradually beat in barely warm melted chocolate until combined. Using metal spoon, gently fold in combined cream and liqueur.
3 Pour mixture into pan. Place pan in baking dish; pour enough boiling water into dish to come halfway up side of pan. Bake about 30 minutes. Cover pan loosely with foil; bake about 30 minutes. Discard foil; remove pan from dish, cool cake in pan.
4 Turn cake onto serving plate, cover; refrigerate overnight. Serve dusted with a little sifted cocoa, if you like. Goes well served with a raspberry coulis and fresh raspberries.

prep + cook time 1 hour 15 minutes (+ cooling & refrigeration)
serves 12
tip We used Cointreau in this recipe, you could use any orange-flavoured liqueur you prefer.

hazelnut mud cake with fudge frosting

360g dark chocolate,
  chopped coarsely
225g butter, chopped coarsely
¾ cup (165g) firmly packed
  brown sugar
¾ cup (180ml) water
¾ cup (110g) plain flour
¼ cup (35g) self-raising flour
½ cup (50g) ground hazelnuts
2 eggs
⅓ cup (80ml) hazelnut-flavoured
  liqueur

fudge frosting
45g butter, chopped coarsely
1 tablespoon water
⅓ cup (75g) firmly packed
  brown sugar
2 tablespoons hazelnut-flavoured
  liqueur
1 cup (160g) icing sugar
2 tablespoons cocoa powder

1 Preheat oven to 150°C/130°C fan-forced. Grease deep 20cm-round cake pan; line base and side with baking paper.
2 Stir chocolate, butter, sugar and the water in medium saucepan over low heat until smooth. Cool 15 minutes. Stir in sifted flours, ground hazelnuts, eggs and liqueur.
3 Pour mixture into pan; bake about 1 hour 35 minutes. Stand cake in pan 5 minutes; turn, top-side up, onto wire rack to cool.
4 Meanwhile, make fudge frosting. Spread cake with frosting.
fudge frosting Stir butter, the water and brown sugar in small saucepan over low heat until sugar dissolves. Remove from heat; stir in liqueur. Sift icing sugar and cocoa into small bowl; gradually stir in hot butter mixture until smooth. Cover; refrigerate about 15 minutes or until frosting thickens. Beat frosting with a wooden spoon until spreadable.

prep + cook time 2 hours (+ cooling) **serves** 12
tip We used Frangelico for this recipe, but you can use any hazelnut or chocolate-flavoured liqueur you like.

gâteau opera

4 eggs
1 1/4 cups (150g) ground almonds
1 cup (160g) icing sugar
1/3 cup (50g) plain flour
25g unsalted butter, melted
4 egg whites
1 tablespoon caster sugar
coffee butter cream
1/4 cup (60ml) milk
1/4 cup (55g) brown sugar
2 teaspoons instant coffee granules
1 egg yolk
125g unsalted butter, softened

coffee syrup
1/3 cup (80ml) boiling water
2 tablespoons caster sugar
1 tablespoon instant coffee
granules
ganache
160g dark eating chocolate,
chopped coarsely
1/3 cup (80ml) cream
glaze
50g unsalted butter, chopped
75g dark eating chocolate

1 Preheat oven to 220°C/200°C fan-forced. Grease two 25cm x 30cm swiss roll pans; line with baking paper, extending paper 5cm above sides.
2 Beat eggs, ground almonds and sifted icing sugar in small bowl with electric mixer until creamy; beat in flour. Transfer to large bowl; stir in butter. Beat egg whites in small bowl with electric mixer until soft peaks form; add caster sugar, beating until sugar dissolves. Fold into almond mixture, in two batches. Divide mixture between pans; bake 7 minutes. Cool.
3 Make coffee butter cream, coffee syrup, and ganache.
4 Cut each cake into a 20cm x 25cm rectangle and a 10cm x 25cm rectangle. Place one of the large cake rectangles on baking-paper-lined tray; brush with half the syrup then spread cake with half the butter cream. Refrigerate 10 minutes. Top butter cream with two small cake rectangles, side-by-side. Brush tops with remaining syrup; spread with ganache. Top with remaining cake; refrigerate 10 minutes. Spread remaining butter cream over top of cake; refrigerate 3 hours.
5 Make glaze; quickly spread over cake. Refrigerate 30 minutes or until set.
coffee butter cream Stir milk, sugar and coffee in small saucepan until sugar dissolves. Whisk yolk in small bowl; whisk in hot milk mixture. Return custard to pan; stir over heat, without boiling until thickened slightly. Cool. Beat butter in small bowl until light and fluffy; beat in custard.
coffee syrup Combine ingredients in small bowl.
ganache Stir ingredients in small heatproof bowl over small saucepan of simmering water until smooth. Refrigerate until spreadable.
glaze Stir ingredients in small heatproof bowl over small saucepan of simmering water until smooth. Use while warm.
prep + cook time 1 hour (+ cooling & refrigeration) **serves** 24

new york cheesecake

250g plain sweet biscuits
125g butter, melted
filling
750g cream cheese, softened
2 teaspoons finely grated orange rind
1 teaspoon finely grated lemon rind
1 cup (220g) caster sugar
3 eggs
¾ cup (180g) sour cream
¼ cup (60ml) lemon juice
sour cream topping
1 cup (240g) sour cream
2 tablespoons caster sugar
2 teaspoons lemon juice

1 Process biscuits until fine. Add butter; process until combined.
Press mixture over base and side of 24cm springform tin. Place tin
on oven tray; refrigerate 30 minutes.
2 Preheat oven to 180°C/160°C fan-forced.
3 Make filling by beating cheese, rinds and sugar in medium bowl
with electric mixer until smooth. Beat in eggs, one at a time. Beat in
cream and juice.
4 Pour filling into tin; bake 1¼ hours. Remove from oven; cool 15 minutes.
5 Make sour cream topping by combining ingredients in small bowl;
spread over cheesecake.
6 Bake cheesecake 20 minutes; cool in oven with door ajar. Refrigerate
cheesecake 3 hours or overnight.

prep + cook time 1 hour 40 minutes (+ refrigeration) **serves** 12

raspberry brownie ice-cream cake

1 litre vanilla ice-cream, softened
150g frozen raspberries
125g butter, chopped coarsely
200g dark eating chocolate, chopped coarsely
½ cup (110g) caster sugar
2 eggs
1¼ cups (185g) plain flour
150g milk eating chocolate, chopped coarsely
1 tablespoon icing sugar

1 Line deep 23cm-round cake pan with plastic wrap, extending wrap so it will cover pan. Combine ice-cream and raspberries in medium bowl. Spoon ice-cream into pan; smooth surface. Fold plastic wrap over to enclose. Freeze 3 hours or until firm.
2 Preheat oven to 160°C/140°C fan-forced. Remove ice-cream from pan, still wrapped in plastic; place on tray. Return to freezer.
3 Grease same pan; line base and side with baking paper.
4 Stir butter, dark chocolate and sugar in medium saucepan over low heat until smooth. Cool 10 minutes. Stir in eggs, sifted flour and milk chocolate.
5 Spread mixture into pan; bake about 30 minutes. Cool in pan.
6 Split brownie in half. Sandwich ice-cream cake between brownie slices; serve immediately, dusted with sifted icing sugar.

prep + cook time 1 hour (+ freezing) **serves** 12

cardamom orange mousse cakes

50g dark eating chocolate, melted
25g unsalted butter, melted
125g butternut snap biscuits
25g unsalted butter, melted, extra
1 teaspoon finely grated orange rind
¼ teaspoon ground cardamom
orange mousse
300ml thickened cream
150g dark eating chocolate, chopped coarsely
1 teaspoon finely grated orange rind
¼ teaspoon ground cardamom
orange syrup
⅔ cup (160ml) orange juice
¼ cup (55g) caster sugar
2 tablespoons finely shredded orange rind

1 Make orange mousse.
2 Grease 12-hole (¼-cup/60ml) mini cheesecake pan with removable bases; line bases with baking paper.
3 Combine chocolate and butter, spoon into holes; cool 5 minutes.
4 Process biscuits until fine. Add extra butter, rind and cardamom; process until combined. Spoon mixture into pan holes; press firmly over chocolate bases.
5 Spoon mousse into pan holes; refrigerate overnight.
6 Make orange syrup. Serve mousse cakes with orange syrup.
orange mousse Stir ingredients in small heatproof bowl over small saucepan of simmering water until smooth. Refrigerate 30 minutes or until cool. Beat mousse with electric mixer 2 minutes or until mixture changes to a paler colour. Do not overbeat or mixture will curdle.
orange syrup Stir juice and sugar in small saucepan, over heat, without boiling, until sugar dissolves. Add rind; bring to the boil. Reduce heat; simmer, uncovered, about 10 minutes or until thickened slightly. Cool.

prep + cook time 1 hour (+ refrigeration) **makes** 12

sticky banana cakes with butterscotch sauce

You need about 2 large overripe bananas (460g) to get the required
amount of mashed banana.

125g butter, softened
⅔ cup (150g) firmly packed brown sugar
2 eggs
1½ cups (225g) self-raising flour
1 teaspoon mixed spice
1 cup mashed banana
¼ cup (60g) sour cream
¼ cup (60ml) milk
2 tablespoons brown sugar, extra
1 large banana (230g), sliced thinly
butterscotch sauce
½ cup (110g) firmly packed brown sugar
⅔ cup (160ml) cream
50g butter

1 Preheat oven to 180°C/160°C fan-forced. Grease eight holes of
two six-hole (¾-cup/180ml) texas muffin pans.
2 Beat butter and sugar in small bowl with electric mixer until light
and fluffy. Beat in eggs, one at a time. Transfer mixture to large bowl;
stir in sifted flour and spice, mashed banana, sour cream and milk,
in two batches.
3 Sprinkle extra sugar in pan holes; cover bases of pan holes with
sliced banana. Spoon cake mixture into pan holes; bake 30 minutes.
4 Meanwhile, make butterscotch sauce.
5 Turn puddings, top-side down, onto serving plates; serve warm with
butterscotch sauce.
butterscotch sauce Stir ingredients in small saucepan over heat,
without boiling, until sugar dissolves. Simmer, stirring, about 3 minutes or
until sauce thickens slightly.

prep + cook time 45 minutes **makes** 8

sticky date cake with butterscotch sauce

3¾ cups (525g) dried pitted dates
3 cups (750ml) hot water
2 teaspoons bicarbonate of soda
185g butter, softened
2¼ cups (500g) firmly packed
  brown sugar
6 eggs
3 cups (450g) self-raising flour
½ cup (55g) coarsely chopped
  walnuts
½ cup (60g) coarsely chopped
  pecans

butterscotch sauce
2 cups (440g) firmly packed
  brown sugar
2 cups (500ml) thickened cream
250g butter, chopped

1 Preheat oven to 180°C/160°C fan-forced. Grease 26cm x 36cm baking dish; line base and long sides of dish with two layers baking paper, extending paper 5cm above edges.

2 Combine dates and the water in medium saucepan; bring to the boil. Remove from heat; stir in soda. Stand 5 minutes then blend or process date mixture until smooth.

3 Beat butter and sugar in large bowl with electric mixer until light and fluffy. Beat in eggs, one at a time. Stir date mixture and sifted flour into egg mixture; spread mixture into dish. Sprinkle with nuts.

4 Bake cake about 50 minutes. Stand cake in dish 10 minutes; turn, top-side up, onto wire rack to cool.

5 Meanwhile, make butterscotch sauce. Brush surface of hot cake with ⅓ cup of the hot butterscotch sauce. Serve with remaining sauce.

butterscotch sauce Stir ingredients in medium saucepan over heat, without boiling, until sugar dissolves; bring to the boil. Reduce heat; simmer 3 minutes.

prep + cook time 1 hour 10 minutes **serves** 20

chocolate sticky date cakes

120g dark eating chocolate, melted
1¾ cups (250g) seeded dried dates
1 teaspoon bicarbonate of soda
1 cup (250ml) boiling water
60g butter, chopped
¾ cup (165g) firmly packed brown sugar
2 eggs
1 cup (150g) self-raising flour
80g dark eating chocolate, chopped coarsely
chocolate butterscotch sauce
½ cup (110g) firmly packed brown sugar
⅔ cup (160ml) cream
50g butter
1 tablespoon cocoa powder, sifted

1 Preheat oven to 180°C/160°C fan-forced. Grease six-hole (¾-cup/
180ml) texas muffin pan; line bases with baking paper.
2 Spread melted chocolate over base of each pan hole; refrigerate
until set.
3 Meanwhile, combine dates, soda and the water in food processor, put
lid in position; stand 5 minutes. Process until smooth. Add butter and
sugar; process until combined. Add eggs and flour; pulse until combined.
Stir in chopped chocolate.
4 Spoon mixture into pan holes; bake about 15 minutes. Stand cakes
in pan 2 minutes; turn onto wire rack to cool slightly. Remove paper.
5 Make chocolate butterscotch sauce.
6 Serve warm cakes drizzled with sauce and whipped cream, if you like.
chocolate butterscotch sauce Stir ingredients in medium saucepan
over heat, without boiling, until sugar dissolves; bring to the boil. Remove
from heat.

prep + cook time 40 minutes **makes** 6

vanilla spice cheesecake

¾ cup (110g) plain flour
¼ teaspoon ground cinnamon
pinch ground nutmeg
⅓ cup (75g) caster sugar
80g butter, melted
½ teaspoon vanilla extract
⅓ cup (45g) roasted hazelnuts,
    chopped coarsely
¼ cup (80g) apricot jam,
    warmed, strained

filling
1 vanilla bean
250g cream cheese, softened
500g ricotta cheese
2 tablespoons lemon juice
⅔ cup (150g) caster sugar
2 eggs

1 Grease 24cm springform tin.
2 Sift flour, spices and sugar into medium bowl; stir in butter, extract and nuts. Press mixture over base of tin. Place tin on oven tray; refrigerate 30 minutes.
3 Preheat oven to 180°C/160°C fan-forced.
4 Bake base about 20 minutes or until browned lightly. Spread with jam. Reduce oven to 150°C/130°C fan-forced.
5 Make filling by splitting vanilla bean in half lengthways; scrape seeds into medium bowl. Add cheeses, juice and half the sugar; beat, with electric mixer until combined.
6 Beat remaining sugar and eggs in small bowl with electric mixer about 5 minutes or until thick and creamy; fold into cheese mixture.
7 Pour filling into tin; bake about 35 minutes. Cool cheesecake in oven with door ajar. Refrigerate cheesecake 3 hours or overnight.

prep + cook time 1 hour 20 minutes (+ refrigeration) **serves** 12

berry meringue torte

6 egg whites
1 cup (220g) caster sugar
1 tablespoon cornflour
600ml thickened cream
⅓ cup (75g) caster sugar, extra
300g fresh blueberries
360g fresh raspberries
250g strawberries, sliced thinly
2 tablespoons icing sugar

mixed berry coulis
120g fresh blueberries
120g fresh raspberries
120g fresh blackberries
¼ cup (55g) caster sugar

1 Preheat oven to 180°C/160°C fan-forced. Grease three oven trays; line with baking paper. Mark 23cm-diameter circle on each piece of paper.
2 Beat egg whites in medium bowl with electric mixer until soft peaks form. Add sugar, 1 tablespoon at a time, beating until sugar dissolves between each addition; beat in cornflour. Spread meringue over circles on trays.
3 Bake meringues 10 minutes. Reduce oven to 150°C/130°C fan-forced; bake further 15 minutes. Cool meringues in oven with door ajar.
4 Meanwhile, make mixed berry coulis.
5 Beat cream and extra sugar in small bowl with electric mixer until firm peaks form.
6 Place one meringue on serving plate; flatten slightly. Layer with half of the cream mixture then top with half of the combined berries. Repeat layering with a second meringue, remaining cream and three-quarters of remaining berries, reserving remaining berries. Cover torte; refrigerate 3 hours.
7 Top meringue torte with reserved berries, dust with sifted icing sugar; serve with berry coulis.
mixed berry coulis Simmer ingredients in medium saucepan, uncovered, over low heat, about 10 minutes or until berries have softened. Push mixture through sieve into medium bowl; cool. Discard seeds.

prep + cook time 45 minutes (+ cooling & refrigeration) **serves** 8

ginger and lime cake

250g butter, chopped coarsely
½ cup (110g) firmly packed
  dark brown sugar
⅔ cup (230g) golden syrup
12cm piece fresh ginger (60g),
  grated
¾ cup (180ml) cream
2 eggs
1 cup (150g) plain flour
1 cup (150g) self-raising flour
½ teaspoon bicarbonate of soda
1 cup (50g) flaked coconut

lime syrup
½ cup (125ml) lime juice
½ cup (125ml) water
½ cup (110g) caster sugar
mascarpone cream
250g mascarpone cheese
300ml thickened cream
2 tablespoons icing sugar
2 teaspoons finely grated
  lime rind

1 Preheat oven to 180°C/160°C fan-forced. Grease deep 22cm-round cake pan; line base and side with baking paper.

2 Melt butter in medium saucepan; remove pan from heat. Stir in sugar, golden syrup and ginger; stir until sugar dissolves. Whisk in cream, eggs and sifted flours and soda.

3 Pour mixture into pan; bake about 40 minutes.

4 Meanwhile, make lime syrup.

5 Pierce hot cake, still in pan, all over with skewer; drizzle hot syrup over hot cake. Cover; refrigerate about 3 hours or until cold.

6 Meanwhile, make mascarpone cream.

7 Remove cake from pan; line base and side of same cleaned pan with plastic wrap. Split cake into three layers; return one layer of cake to pan. Spread layer with 1 cup of the mascarpone cream; repeat with second cake layer and another 1 cup of mascarpone cream, then top with third cake layer. Cover cake; refrigerate 2 hours. Refrigerate remaining mascarpone cream until required.

8 Remove cake from pan to serving plate, spread remaining mascarpone cream all over cake; press coconut onto side of cake.

lime syrup Stir ingredients in small saucepan over heat, without boiling, until sugar dissolves; bring to the boil. Reduce heat; simmer, uncovered, without stirring, 2 minutes.

mascarpone cream Whisk ingredients in small bowl until soft peaks form. Refrigerate until required.

prep + cook time 1 hour 30 minutes (+ refrigeration) **serves** 12

cheesecake brownies

125g butter, chopped
150g dark eating chocolate, chopped coarsely
1 egg
⅔ cup (150g) caster sugar
¾ cup (110g) plain flour
¼ cup (35g) self-raising flour
topping
250g cream cheese, softened
1 teaspoon vanilla extract
⅓ cup (75g) caster sugar
1 egg
½ cup (125ml) cream

1 Preheat oven to 180°C/160°C fan-forced. Grease deep 19cm-square cake pan; line base and sides with baking paper, extending paper 5cm above sides.
2 Stir butter and chocolate in small saucepan over low heat until smooth. Cool.
3 Beat egg and sugar in small bowl with electric mixer until thick and creamy. Stir in chocolate mixture and sifted flours.
4 Spread mixture into pan; bake 10 minutes.
5 Make topping.
6 Pour topping over brownie base; bake about 15 minutes. Cool in oven with door ajar. Refrigerate brownies 3 hours.
topping Beat cheese, extract, sugar and egg in small bowl with electric mixer until smooth; beat in cream.

prep + cook time 45 minutes (+ refrigeration) **serves** 12

spiced fig and orange cheesecake

½ cup (80g) brazil nuts
125g plain sweet biscuits
80g butter, melted
1 cup (250ml) orange juice
1¼ cups (250g) finely chopped dried figs
1 cinnamon stick
pinch ground clove
filling
250g cream cheese, softened
1 tablespoon finely grated orange rind
¾ cup (165g) caster sugar
1 cup (250g) mascarpone cheese
2 eggs, separated

1 Grease 22cm springform tin.
2 Process nuts and biscuits until fine. Add butter; process until combined. Press mixture over base of tin. Place tin on oven tray; refrigerate 30 minutes.
3 Preheat oven to 160°C/140°C fan-forced.
4 Combine juice, figs, cinnamon and cloves in small saucepan; simmer, uncovered, 10 minutes or until most of the juice has been absorbed. Discard cinnamon stick. Spread fig mixture over crumb base in tin.
5 Make filling by beating cream cheese, rind and sugar in medium bowl with electric mixer until smooth. Add mascarpone and yolks; beat only until combined. Beat egg whites in small bowl with electric mixer until soft peaks form; fold into cheese mixture.
6 Pour filling over fig mixture; bake about 1¼ hours. Cool in oven with door ajar. Refrigerate 3 hours or overnight. Serve dusted with sifted icing sugar, if you like.

prep + cook time 1 hour 40 minutes (+ refrigeration) **serves** 12

glossary

allspice also called pimento or jamaican pepper; so-named because it tastes like a combination of nutmeg, cumin, clove and cinnamon. Available whole (a dark-brown berry the size of a pea) or ground.

almonds flat, pointy-tipped nuts having a pitted brown shell enclosing a creamy white kernel which is covered by a brown skin.

blanched brown skins removed.

essence made with almond oil and alcohol or another agent.

flaked paper-thin slices.

ground also known as almond meal; nuts are powdered to a coarse flour texture for use in baking or as a thickening agent.

slivered small pieces cut lengthways.

vienna toffee-coated almonds.

baking paper also known as parchment, silicon paper or non-stick baking paper; not to be confused with greaseproof or waxed paper. Used to line pans before cooking and baking; also to make piping bags.

baking powder a raising agent consisting mainly of two parts cream of tartar to one part bicarbonate of soda (baking soda).

beetroot also called red beets; firm, round root vegetable.

bicarbonate of soda also known as baking soda; a mild alkali used as a leavening agent in baking.

brandy short for brandywine, the translation of the Dutch "brandwijn", burnt wine. A general term for a liqueur distilled from wine grapes (usually white), it is used as the basis for many sweet-to-dry spirits made with fruits. Cognac and Armagnac are two of the finest aged brandies available.

butter we use salted butter unless stated otherwise; 125g is equal to 1 stick (4oz). Unsalted or "sweet" butter has no added salt.

buttermilk originally the term given to the slightly sour liquid left after butter was churned from cream, today it is made similarly to yogurt. Sold alongside milk products in supermarkets. Despite the implication of its name, it is low in fat.

cardamom a spice native to India and used extensively in its cuisine; can be purchased in pod, seed or ground form. Has a distinctive aromatic, sweetly rich flavour and is one of the world's most expensive spices. Used to flavour curries, rice dishes, sweet desserts and cakes.

cheese

cream commonly known as philadelphia or philly; a soft cow-milk cheese with a fat content ranging from 14 to 33 per cent.

mascarpone an Italian fresh cultured-cream product made in much the same way as yogurt. Whiteish to creamy yellow in colour, with a buttery-rich, luscious texture. Soft, creamy and spreadable, it is used in many Italian desserts and as an accompaniment to a dessert of fresh fruit.

ricotta a soft, sweet, moist, white cow-milk cheese with a low fat content (8.5 per cent) and a slightly grainy texture. Its name roughly translates as "cooked again" and refers to ricotta's manufacture from a whey that is itself a by-product of other cheese making.

cherry small, soft stone fruit varying in colour from yellow to dark red. Sweet cherries are eaten whole and in desserts while sour cherries such as the morello variety are used for jams, preserves, pies and savoury dishes.

glacé also called candied cherries; boiled in heavy sugar syrup and then dried. Used in cakes, breads and sweets.

chocolate

cherry ripe dark chocolate bar made with coconut and cherries; standard size bar weighs 55g.

Choc Bits also known as chocolate chips or chocolate morsels; available in milk, white and dark chocolate. Made of cocoa liquor, cocoa butter, sugar and an emulsifier; hold their shape in baking and are ideal for decorating.

choc Melts small discs of compounded milk, white or dark chocolate ideal for melting and moulding.

couverture a term used to describe a fine quality, very rich chocolate high in both cocoa butter and cocoa liquor. Requires tempering when used to coat but not if used in baking, mousses or fillings.

dark cooking also known as compounded chocolate; good for cooking as it doesn't require tempering and sets at room temperature. Made with vegetable fat instead

of cocoa butter so it lacks the rich, buttery flavour of eating chocolate. Cocoa butter is the most expensive component in chocolate, so the substitution of a vegetable fat means that compounded chocolate is much cheaper to produce.

dark eating also known as semi-sweet or luxury chocolate; made of a high percentage of cocoa liquor and cocoa butter, and little added sugar. Unless stated otherwise, we use dark eating chocolate in this book as it's ideal for use in desserts and cakes.

milk eating most popular eating chocolate, mild and very sweet; similar in make-up to dark with the difference being the addition of milk solids.

white eating contains no cocoa solids but derives its sweet flavour from cocoa butter. Very sensitive to heat.

chocolate hazelnut spread we use Nutella. It was initially developed when chocolate was hard to source during World War 2; hazelnuts were added to extend the chocolate supply.

cinnamon available in the piece (sticks or quills) and ground into powder; one of the

world's most common spices, used universally as a flavouring for both sweet and savoury foods.

cloves dried flower buds of a tropical tree; can be used whole or in ground form. They have a strong scent and taste so should be used sparingly.

cocoa powder also known as unsweetened cocoa; cocoa beans (cacao seeds) that have been fermented, roasted, shelled, ground into powder then cleared of most of the fat content.

coconut

desiccated concentrated, dried, unsweetened and finely shredded coconut flesh.

essence synthetically made from flavouring, oil and alcohol.

flaked dried flaked coconut flesh.

shredded unsweetened thin strips of dried coconut flesh.

corella pears are miniature dessert pears with pale flesh and a sweet, mild flavour.

cornflour also known as cornstarch. Available made from corn or wheat (wheaten cornflour, gluten-free, gives a lighter texture in cakes); used as a thickening agent.

corn syrup a sweet syrup made by heating

cornstarch with water under pressure. It comes in light and dark types and is used in baking and in confectionery.

cream

pouring also known as pure cream. It has no additives, and contains a minimum fat content of 35 per cent.

thickened a whipping cream that contains a thickener. Has a minimum fat content of 35 per cent.

cream of tartar the acid ingredient in baking powder; added to confectionery mixtures to help prevent sugar from crystallising. Keeps frostings creamy and improves volume when beating egg whites.

custard powder instant mixture used to make pouring custard; similar to North American instant pudding mixes.

dates fruit of the date palm tree, eaten fresh or dried, on their own or in prepared dishes. About 4cm to 6cm in length, oval and plump, thin-skinned, with a honey-sweet flavour and sticky texture.

dried cranberries have the same slightly sour, succulent flavour as fresh cranberries. Can often be substituted for or with other dried fruit in most recipes.

Available in most supermarkets.

dried currants dried tiny, almost black raisins so-named from the grape type native to Corinth, Greece; most often used in jams, jellies and sauces). These are not the same as fresh currants, which are the fruit of a plant in the gooseberry family.

eggs we use large chicken eggs (60g) in our recipes unless stated otherwise. If a recipe calls for raw or barely cooked eggs, exercise caution if there is a salmonella problem in your area.

figs fresh figs are best eaten in peak season, at the height of summer. They vary in skin and flesh colour according to type not ripeness. When ripe, figs should be unblemished and bursting with flesh; nectar beads at the base indicate when a fig is at its best.

five-spice although the ingredients vary from country to country, five-spice is usually a fragrant mixture of ground cinnamon, cloves, star anise, sichuan pepper and fennel seeds. Used in Chinese and other Asian cooking; available from most supermarkets or Asian food shops.

flour

plain also known as all-purpose; unbleached wheat flour is the best for baking.

rice very fine, almost powdery, gluten-free flour; made from ground white rice.

self-raising all-purpose plain or wholemeal flour with baking powder and salt added; can be made at home with plain or wholemeal flour sifted with baking powder in the proportion of 1 cup flour to 2 teaspoons baking powder.

wholemeal also called wholewheat flour; milled with the wheat germ so is higher in fibre and more nutritional than white flour. Available plain and self-raising.

food colouring vegetable-based substance available in liquid, paste or gel form.

fruit mince also called mincemeat. A mixture of dried fruits such as raisins, sultanas and candied peel, nuts, spices, apple, brandy or rum. Is used as a filling for cakes, puddings and fruit mince pies.

gelatine a thickening agent. Available in sheet form (leaf gelatine) or as a powder — 3 teaspoons powdered gelatine (8g or one sachet) is roughly equivalent to four gelatine leaves.

ginger

fresh also known as green or root ginger; the thick gnarled root of a tropical plant.

glacé fresh ginger root preserved in sugar syrup; crystallised ginger can be substituted if rinsed with warm water and dried before using.

ground also known as powdered ginger; used as a flavouring in cakes, pies and puddings but cannot be substituted for fresh ginger.

ginger wine a beverage that is 14 per cent alcohol by volume, has the piquant taste of fresh ginger. Available at hotels and bottle shops.

glacé fruit fruit such as pineapple, apricots, peaches and pears that are cooked in a heavy sugar syrup then dried.

golden syrup a by-product of refined sugarcane; pure maple syrup or honey can be substituted.

greasing pans use butter, margarine, oil or cooking-oil spray to grease baking pans; over-greasing can cause food to overbrown. Use absorbent paper or a pastry brush to spread the oil or butter over the pan. Try covering your hand with a small plastic bag then swiping it into the butter or margarine.

hazelnuts also called filberts; plump, grape-size, rich, sweet nut having a brown inedible skin that is removed by rubbing heated nuts together vigorously in a tea-towel.

ground is made by grounding the hazelnuts to a coarse flour texture.

honey honey sold in a squeezable container is not suitable for the recipes in this book.

jam also known as preserve or conserve.

jelly crystals a combination of sugar, gelatine, colours and flavours; when dissolved in water, the solution sets as firm jelly.

jersey caramels a softish confectionery, caramel in colour with a white stripe in the middle. Available in supermarkets.

lemon butter a commercially prepared lemon curd or lemon-flavoured spread.

liqueur

coffee-flavoured vodka or rum-based liqueur; we use Kahlua.

hazelnut-flavoured we use frangelico.

kirsch cherry-flavoured liqueur.

orange-flavoured brandy-based liqueur such as Grand Marnier or Cointreau.

macadamias native to Australia; fairly large, slightly soft, buttery rich nut. Should always be stored in the fridge to prevent their high oil content turning them rancid.

mandarin also known as tangerine; a small, loose-skinned, easy-to-peel, sweet and juicy citrus fruit, prized for its eating qualities more than for juicing. Segments in a light syrup are available canned.

maple-flavoured syrup is made from sugar cane and is also known as golden or pancake syrup. It is not a substitute for pure maple syrup.

maple syrup distilled from the sap of sugar maple trees found only in Canada and about ten states in the USA. Most often eaten with pancakes or waffles, but also used as an ingredient in baking or in preparing desserts. Maple-flavoured syrup or pancake syrup is not an adequate substitute for the real thing.

milk we use full-cream homogenised milk unless stated otherwise.

sweetened condensed a canned milk product consisting of milk with more than half the water content removed and sugar added to the remaining milk.

top 'n' fill caramel a canned milk product made of condensed milk that has been boiled to a caramel.

mixed dried fruit a combination of sultanas, raisins, currants, mixed peel and cherries.

mixed peel candied citrus peel.

mixed spice a classic mixture generally containing caraway, allspice, coriander, cumin, nutmeg and ginger, although cinnamon and other spices can be added. It is used with fruit and in cakes.

muscat also known as muscatel; refers to both the grape variety and the sweet dessert wine made from them. The grape is superb eaten fresh; when dried, its distinctively musty flavour goes well with cheese, chocolate, pork and game. In winemaking, the grape is used for Italian Asti Spumante, a range of Australian fortifieds, Metaxa from Greece and so on.

nutmeg a strong and very pungent spice ground from the dried nut of an evergreen tree native to Indonesia. Usually found ground

but the flavour is more intense from a whole nut, available from spice shops, so it's best to grate your own. Found in mixed spice mixtures.

oil

cooking spray we use a cholesterol-free cooking spray made from canola oil.

vegetable any of a number of oils sourced from plant rather than animal fats.

orange blossom water also known as orange flower water; a concentrated flavouring made from orange blossoms. Available from Middle-Eastern food stores and some supermarkets and delicatessens. Cannot be substituted with citrus flavourings, as the taste is completely different.

pecans native to the US and now grown locally; pecans are golden brown, buttery and rich. Good in savoury as well as sweet dishes; walnuts are a good substitute.

pine nuts also known as pignoli; not in fact a nut but a small, cream-coloured kernel from pine cones. They are best roasted before use to bring out the flavour.

pistachios green, delicately flavoured nuts inside hard off-white

shells. Available salted or unsalted in their shells; you can also get them shelled.

poppy seeds small, dried, bluish-grey seeds of the poppy plant, with a crunchy texture and a nutty flavour. Can be purchased whole or ground in most supermarkets.

quince yellow-skinned fruit with hard texture and astringent, tart taste; eaten cooked or as a preserve. Long, slow cooking makes the flesh a deep rose pink.

raisins dried sweet grapes (traditionally muscatel grapes).

ready-made white icing also known as soft icing, ready-to-roll and prepared fondant. Available from the baking section in most supermarkets.

rhubarb classified as a vegetable, is eaten as a fruit and therefore considered one. Leaves must be removed before cooking as they can contain traces of poison; the edible crisp, pink-red stalks are chopped and cooked.

rosewater extract made from crushed rose petals; used for its aromatic quality.

roasting/toasting nuts and dried coconut can be roasted in the oven to restore their fresh flavour and release their aromatic essential oils. Spread them evenly onto an oven tray then roast in a moderate oven for about 5 minutes. Desiccated coconut, pine nuts and sesame seeds roast more evenly if stirred over low heat in a heavy-based frying pan; their natural oils will help turn them golden brown.

rum we use a dark underproof rum for a more subtle flavour in cooking. White rum is almost colourless, sweet and used mostly in mixed drinks.

semolina coarsely ground flour milled from durum wheat; the flour used in making gnocchi, pasta and couscous.

sherry fortified wine consumed as an aperitif or used in cooking. Sherries differ in colour and flavour; sold as fino (light, dry), amontillado (medium sweet, dark) and oloroso (full-bodied, very dark).

sour cream thick, commercially-cultured sour cream with a minimum fat content of 35 per cent.

star anise a dried star-shaped pod whose seeds have an astringent aniseed flavour.

sugar we use coarse, granulated table sugar, also called crystal sugar, unless stated otherwise.

brown an extremely soft, fine granulated sugar retaining molasses for its characteristic colour and flavour.

caster also known as superfine or finely granulated table sugar. The fine crystals dissolve easily making it perfect for cakes, meringues and desserts.

demarara small-grained golden-coloured crystal sugar.

icing also known as confectioners' sugar or powdered sugar; pulverised granulated sugar crushed together with a small amount (about 3 per cent) of cornflour.

pure icing also known as confectioners' or powdered sugar; does not contain cornflour.

raw natural brown granulated sugar.

vanilla granulated or caster sugar flavoured with a vanilla bean; can be stored indefinitely.

sultanas also called golden raisins; dried seedless white grapes.

tempering the process by which chocolate is melted at a specific temperature that enables it to set with a glossy finish.

treacle thick, dark syrup not unlike molasses; a by-product of sugar refining.

vanilla

bean dried, long, thin pod from a tropical golden orchid grown in central and South America and Tahiti; the minuscule black seeds inside the bean are used to impart a luscious vanilla flavour in baking and desserts.

essence obtained from vanilla beans infused in alcohol and water.

extract obtained from vanilla beans infused in water; a non-alcoholic version of essence.

walnuts as well as being a good source of fibre and healthy oils, nuts contain a range of vitamins, minerals and other beneficial plant components called phytochemicals. Each type of nut has a special make-up and walnuts contain the beneficial omega-3 fatty acids.

wine the adage that you should never cook with wine you wouldn't drink holds true in this book; unless specified otherwise, we use good-quality dry white and red wines in our recipes.

yogurt we use plain full-cream yogurt in our recipes unless stated otherwise.

index

A

almonds
  almond butter cake 26
  dark chocolate and
    almond torte 341
  orange, almond and
    pine nut cake 204
  pear and almond cake
    with passionfruit
    glaze 46
  vanilla pear almond
    cake 353
apple(s)
  caramelised 172
  caramelised apple
    teacakes 172
  custard teacakes 241
  raspberry and apple
    cupcakes 266
  raspberry bread 171
  spiced apple
    scones 334
  streusel cake 148
  streusel muffins 313

B

bananas
  banana butterscotch
    syrup cake 224
  banana cake with
    passionfruit icing 151
  banana caramel
    cupcakes 238
  banana caramel
    layer cake 342
  banana, cranberry
    and macadamia
    muffins 309
  banana cupcakes
    with maple cream
    frosting 242
  banana loaves with
    muesli topping 152
  mini choc-chip
    banana loaves 155
  sticky banana cakes
    with butterscotch
    sauce 370
basic butter cake 13

berries
  apple raspberry
    bread 171
  banana, cranberry
    and macadamia
    muffins 309
  berry cupcakes 262
  blueberry yogurt
    loaf 168
  buttermilk muffins 326
  chocolate raspberry
    brownies 68
  chocolate raspberry
    dessert muffins 322
  lemon and cranberry
    friands 286
  meringue torte 378
  mixed berry cake with
    vanilla bean syrup 227
  mixed berry coulis 378
  orange and blueberry
    syrup cake 216
  raspberry and apple
    cupcakes 266
  raspberry brownie
    ice-cream cake 366
  raspberry swirl cake 183
  strawberry coulis 345
black forest cake 346
black forest cupcakes
  278
boiled fruit cake 140
brandied cherry
  friands 298
brownies
  cheesecake 382
  chocolate raspberry 68
  fig and muscat 76
  raspberry ice-cream,
    cake 366
  triple chocolate 71
butter, golden syrup 334
butter cakes
  almond 26
  basic 13
  butterfly cakes 53, 269

(*butter cakes* continued)
  caramel 10
  cinnamon teacake 25
  coconut cake 41
  coffee caramel cake 49
  coffee walnut
    streusel cake 50
  cream cheese
    lemon cake 34
  kisses 42
  lemon and apricot
    cake 17
  madeira cake 29
  marble cake 33
  orange cake 21
  orange macaroon
    cake 14
  orange marmalade
    cake 22
  passionfruit buttermilk
    cake 45
  pear and almond cake
    with passionfruit
    glaze 46
  pecan and date
    ripple cake 38
  pecan sour cream
    cake 18
  pound cake 37
  pumpkin date cake 30
butter frosting 33, 183
butterfly cakes 53
  mini 269
butterscotch pecan
  muffins 321
butterscotch sauce 370,
  373
  chocolate 374
butterscotch syrup 224

C

candy cupcakes 253
caramel
  banana caramel
    cupcakes 238
  banana caramel layer
    cake 342

(*caramel* continued)
caramel butter cake 10
caramel cake with
whole-spice syrup 212
caramel choc-chip
mud cakes 87
coffee caramel cake 49
icing 10, 167
caramelised apple
teacakes 172
cardamom orange
mousse cakes 369
carrot and orange
cupcakes 245
carrot cake with
lemon cream cheese
frosting 187
celebration fruit cake 196
cheesecake
brownies 382
new york 365
spiced fig and
orange 385
vanilla spice 377
cherry friands, brandied
298
cherry sauce 298
choc-chip banana
loaves, mini 155
choc-chip jaffa muffins
314
choc-hazelnut friands
289
choc muffins, triple 317
choc orange ganache 56
chocolate and almond
torte, dark 341
chocolate butter cream,
338
chocolate buttermilk
cream 84
chocolate butterscotch
sauce 374
chocolate cakes
caramel choc-chip
mud cakes 87
choc-cherry cake 91

(*chocolate cakes*
continued)
chocolate, apricot and
hazelnut cake 84
chocolate beetroot
cake 95
chocolate fudge
cake 83
chocolate fudge mud
cakes 250
chocolate ginger
cupcakes 281
chocolate orange
fudge cake 56
chocolate raspberry
brownies 68
chocolate sponge 126
chocolate sticky
date cakes 92, 374
chocolate velvet
cake 80
dark chocolate and
almond torte 341
easy chocolate cake 72
family chocolate
cake 64
fig and muscat
brownies 76
flourless chocolate
cakes with latte
sauce 357
flourless chocolate
dessert cake 345
gluten-free chocolate
cakes 63
gluten-free chocolate
hazelnut cake 96
marbled chocolate
mud cakes 88
mini chocolate
yule logs 75
mississippi mud cake 99
rich chocolate
fruit cake 192
rum and raisin
chocolate cake 67
sacher torte 60

(*chocolate cakes*
continued)
sour cream chocolate
cake 59
triple chocolate
brownies 71
white christmas
mud cakes 79
chocolate fudge
frosting 250
chocolate ganache 75,
95, 270
dark 88, 192, 281
white 88
chocolate icing 60, 63,
72, 269
chocolate raspberry
brownies 68
chocolate raspberry
dessert muffins 322
chocolate roll, grated 102
chocolate rose leaf
decorations 281
chocolate satin icing 91
chocolate yule logs,
mini 75
christmas muffins 305
christmas star
cupcakes 273
cinnamon and walnut
syrup cake 219
cinnamon teacake 25
citrus cupcakes 282
cloud cupcakes 246
coconut
coconut and pineapple
friands 301
coconut cake 41
coconut cherry heart
cupcakes 270
coconut ice frosting 41
crust 143
lime coconut syrup
cake 211
meringue 265
topping 160

coffee
coffee and walnut
friands 294
coffee butter cream 362
coffee caramel cake 49
coffee walnut
streusel cake 50
espresso syrup
cake 232
icing 126
latte sauce 357
rich mocha gâteau 338
syrup 362
cream cheese frosting
262
lemon 187, 254, 257
cream cheese
fruit cake 184
cream cheese lemon
cake 34
cupcakes
apple custard
teacakes 241
banana caramel 238
berry 262
black forest 278
candy 253
carrot and orange 245
chocolate fudge
mud cakes 250
chocolate ginger 281
christmas star 273
citrus 282
cloud 246
coconut cherry
heart 270
florentine 249
lemon meringue 265
mini butterfly cakes
269
orange blossom
cakes 261
patty cakes with
glacé icing 258
raspberry and apple
266
rocky road 277
sweet violet 257

(cupcakes continued)
turkish delight 274
curd
lemon 265
lemon curd friands 290
passionfruit 113
custard 164, 241, 325
apple custard
teacakes 241
rhubarb and custard
muffins 325
rhubarb custard
teacake 164
D
dates
chocolate sticky
date cakes 92
date and pecan roll 176
date muffins with
orange syrup 306
date scones 329
pecan and date
ripple cake 38
pumpkin date cake 30
sticky date cake
with butterscotch
sauce 373
dessert cakes
banana caramel
layer cake 342
berry meringue
torte 378
black forest cake 346
cardamom orange
mousse cakes 369
cheesecake
brownies 382
chocolate sticky date
cakes 92, 374
dark chocolate and
almond torte 341
flourless chocolate
cakes with latte
sauce 357
flourless chocolate
dessert cake 345
flourless fig, pecan and
maple syrup cake 350

(dessert cakes
continued)
gâteau opera 362
ginger and lime cake
381
hazelnut mud cake with
fudge frosting 361
new york cheesecake
365
raspberry brownie
ice-cream cake 366
rich mocha gâteau 338
rich truffle mud cake
358
soft-centred mocha
cakes 349
spiced fig and orange
cheesecake 385
sticky banana cakes
with butterscotch
sauce 370
sticky date cake
with butterscotch
sauce 373
tiramisu cakes 354
vanilla pear almond
cake 353
vanilla spice
cheesecake 377
E
easy chocolate cake 72
espresso syrup 232
espresso syrup cake
232
F
featherlight sponge
cake 110
figs
fig and muscat
brownies 76
fig jam and raisin
rolls 179
flourless fig, pecan and
maple syrup cake 350
spiced fig and orange
cheesecake 385
florentine cupcakes 249
florentine topping 249

flourless chocolate
  dessert cake 345
flourless fig, pecan and
  maple syrup cake 350
fluffy frosting 156, 246
friands
  brandied cherry 298
  choc-hazelnut 289
  coconut and
    pineapple 301
  coffee and walnut 294
  fruit mince 293
  lemon and cranberry
    286
  lemon curd 290
  mandarin and poppy
    seed 297
  pistachio and lime 302
frosting see also glaze;
  icing
  butter 33, 183
  chocolate fudge 250
  coconut ice 41
  cream cheese 262
  fluffy 156, 246
  fudge 64, 96, 361
  lemon cream cheese
    187, 254, 257
  maple cream 242
  vienna cream 42
fruit, sugared 262
fruit and nut topping 147
fruit cakes
  apple raspberry
    bread 171
  apple streusel cake 148
  banana cake with
    passionfruit icing 151
  banana loaves with
    muesli topping 152
  blueberry yogurt
    loaf 168
  boiled fruit cake 140
  caramelised apple
    teacakes 172
  carrot cake with
    lemon cream cheese
    frosting 187

(fruit cakes continued)
  celebration fruit cake
    196
  cream cheese
    fruit cake 184
  date and pecan roll 176
  fig jam and raisin
    rolls 179
  ginger cake with
    caramel icing 167
  gluten-free fruit
    cakes 195
  hummingbird cakes with
    coconut crust 143
  lemon currant loaf 199
  lumberjack cake 160
  mini choc-chip
    banana loaves 155
  mini sultana loaves 163
  moist whole orange
    cake 159
  night-before-christmas
    fruit cake 200
  orange, almond and
    pine nut cake 204
  raisin and honey
    oat bread 175
  raspberry swirl cake 183
  rhubarb custard
    teacake 164
  rich chocolate
    fruit cake 192
  rich fruit cake 191
  rich fruit cake with
    stout 203
  rock cakes 188
  tropical fruit cakes 147
  upside down pear and
    pistachio cake 180
  walnut and prune
    loaf 144
  white christmas
    cake 156
fruit mince friands 293
fudge frosting 64, 96,
  361
  chocolate 250

G
ganache
  choc orange 56
  chocolate 75, 95,
    249, 270
  dark chocolate 88, 192,
    281, 341, 354, 362
  sour cream 59
  white chocolate 88
gâteau opera 362
gâteau, rich mocha 338
genoise sponge 121
ginger
  and lime cake 381
  and pear muffins 318
  cake with caramel
    icing 167
  chocolate ginger
    cupcakes 281
  cream filling 137
  cream roll 137
  powder puffs 118
  sponge 105
  syrup 231
glacé fruit loaf with
  ginger syrup 231
glacé icing 34, 163,
  245, 258, 261
glaze see also frosting;
  icing
  chocolate 80, 362
  passionfruit 46
gluten-free
  chocolate cakes 63
  chocolate hazelnut
    cake 96
  fruit cakes 195
  golden syrup butter 334
grated chocolate roll 102
H
hazelnuts
  choc-hazelnut
    friands 289
  chocolate, apricot and
    hazelnut cake 84
  gluten-free chocolate
    hazelnut cake 96

(*hazelnuts* continued)
hazelnut mud cake with
fudge frosting 361
honey sponge cake 122
hummingbird cakes with
coconut crust 143

I
icing *see also* frosting;
glaze
caramel 10, 167
chocolate 60, 63, 72,
92, 269
chocolate glaze 80
chocolate satin icing 91
coffee 126
glacé 34, 163, 245, 258
lamingtons, for 129,
130
lemon glacé 163
orange 21
orange blossom
glacé icing 261
orange glacé 245
passionfruit 45, 151
passionfruit glaze 46

J
jelly cakes
pineapple 109
strawberry 133

K
kisses 42

L
lamingtons 129
white chocolate 130
latte sauce 357
lemon
and apricot cake 17
and cranberry friands
286
cream cheese
lemon cake 34
curd 265
glacé icing 163
lemon cream cheese
frosting 187, 254, 257
lemon curd friands 290

(*lemon* continued)
lemon currant loaf 199
lemon meringue
cupcakes 265
lemon syrup cake 235
syrup 208, 215, 235
lime
and ricotta syrup
cake 228
ginger and lime
cake 381
lime coconut syrup
cake 211
pistachio and lime
friands 302
syrup 211, 228, 381
loaves & breads
apple raspberry
bread 171
banana loaves with
muesli topping 152
blueberry yogurt
loaf 168
glacé fruit loaf with
ginger syrup 231
lemon currant loaf 199
mini choc-chip
banana loaves 155
mini sultana loaves 163
raisin and honey
oat bread 175
walnut and prune
loaf 144
lumberjack cake 160

M
macaroon
macaroon syrup
cake 208
orange macaroon
cake 14
topping 14
madeira cake 29
malt truffle muffins,
warm 310
mandarin and poppy
seed friands 297

maple cream frosting 242
maple syrup 350
marble cake 33
marbled chocolate
mud cakes 88
mascarpone cream 381
meringue
berry meringue
torte 378
coconut meringue 265
lemon meringue
cupcakes 265
mini choc-chip banana
loaves 155
mini sultana loaves 163
mississippi mud cake
99
mixed berry cake
with vanilla bean
syrup 227
mixed berry coulis 378
mocha cakes, soft-
centred 349
mocha gâteau, rich 338
moist whole orange
cake 159
mud cakes
caramel choc-chip 87
chocolate fudge 250
dark mud cake 88
hazelnut, with fudge
frosting 361
marbled chocolate 88
mississippi 99
rich truffle 358
white christmas 79
white mud cake 88
muesli topping 152, 318
muffins
apple streusel 313
banana, cranberry and
macadamia 309
berry buttermilk 326
butterscotch pecan
321
choc-chip jaffa 314

(*muffins* continued)
chocolate raspberry
dessert 322
christmas 305
date muffins with
orange syrup 306
ginger and pear 318
rhubarb and
custard 325
triple choc 317
warm malt truffle 310

N
new york cheesecake
365
night-before-christmas
fruit cake 200

O
orange
and blueberry syrup
cake 216
cardamom orange
mousse cakes 369
carrot and orange
cupcakes 245
choc orange
ganache 56
chocolate orange
fudge cake 56
cream 118
glacé icing 245, 261
icing 21
moist whole orange
cake 159
orange, almond and
pine nut cake 204
orange blossom
cakes 261
orange cake 21
orange macaroon
cake 14
orange marmalade
cake 22
orange mousse 369
orange poppy seed
syrup cake 223
orange syrup cake 220

(*orange* continued)
spiced fig and orange
cheesecake 385
syrup 216, 223,
306, 369

P
passionfruit
glaze 46
icing 45, 151
passionfruit buttermilk
cake 45
passionfruit curd
sponge cakes 113
patty cakes with
glacé icing 258
pear
and almond cake with
passionfruit glaze 46
ginger and pear
muffins 318
rhubarb and pear
sponge 134
upside down pear and
pistachio cake 180
vanilla pear almond
cake 353
pecan
and date ripple cake 38
butterscotch pecan
muffins 321
date and pecan roll 176
flourless fig, pecan
and maple syrup
cake 350
sour cream cake 18
topping 38
pineapple flowers 254
pineapple
coconut and pineapple
friands 301
flowers 254
hibiscus cupcakes 254
jelly cakes 109
pistachio and lime
friands 302
pistachio honey
cream 117

plum jam scone ring 333
pound cake 37
pumpkin date cake 30
pumpkin scones 330

R
raisin and honey
oat bread 175
raspberry and apple
cupcakes 266
raspberry brownie
ice-cream cake 366
raspberry swirl cake 183
rhubarb
and custard muffins 325
and pear sponge 134
custard teacake 164
rich chocolate
fruit cake 192
rich fruit cake 191
with stout 203
rich mocha gâteau 338
rock cakes 188
rocky road cupcakes 277
rocky road topping 277
rum and raisin
chocolate cake 67

S
sacher torte 60
sauces
butterscotch 370, 373
cherry 298
chocolate butterscotch
374
latte sauce 357
scones
basic 329
date 329
plum jam scone
ring 333
pumpkin 330
spiced apple 334
semolina and yogurt
lemon-syrup cake 215
soft-centred mocha
cakes 349
sour cream
chocolate cake 59

(*sour cream* continued)
ganache 59
pecan sour cream
cake 18
topping 365
spiced apple scones 334
spiced sponge with
pistachio honey
cream 117
sponge cakes
chocolate sponge 126
featherlight 110
genoise sponge 121
ginger cream roll 137
ginger powder
puffs 118
ginger sponge 105
grated chocolate
roll 102
honey 122
lamingtons 129
passionfruit curd
sponge cakes 113
pineapple jelly
cakes 109
rhubarb and pear
sponge 134
spiced sponge with
pistachio honey
cream 117
sponge roll with jam
and cream 114
strawberry jelly
cakes 133
victoria sponge
sandwich 125
wheat-free sponge
106
white chocolate
lamingtons 130
sticky banana cakes
with butterscotch
sauce 370
strawberry coulis 345
strawberry jelly cakes
133

sugar syrup 219
sugared fruit 262
sultana loaves, mini 163
sweet violet cupcakes
257
syrup cakes
banana butterscotch
syrup cake 224
caramel cake with
whole-spice syrup 212
cinnamon and
walnut 219
espresso 232
glacé fruit loaf with
ginger syrup 231
lemon 235
lime and ricotta 228
lime coconut 211
macaroon 208
mixed berry cake
with vanilla bean
syrup 227
orange and
blueberry 216
orange poppy seed 223
orange 220
semolina and yogurt
lemon-syrup cake 215

T
teacakes
apple custard 241
caramelised apple 172
cinnamon 25
rhubarb custard 164
tiramisu cakes 354
topping
apple streusel 148
coconut 160
florentine 249
fruit and nut 147
macaroon 14
muesli 152, 318
pecan 38
rocky road 277
sour cream 365
streusel 148, 313

(*topping* continued)
walnut streusel 50
white christmas 79
triple chocolate
brownies 71
tropical fruit cakes 147
truffle mud cake,
rich 358
truffle muffins,
warm malt 310
turkish delight
cupcakes 274
U
upside down pear and
pistachio cake 180
V
vanilla bean syrup 227
vanilla cream 102
vanilla pear almond
cake 353
vanilla spice
cheesecake 377
victoria sponge
sandwich 125
vienna cream 42
W
walnut
and prune loaf 144
coffee and walnut
friands 294
streusel 50
wheat-free sponge 106
white chocolate
lamingtons 130
white christmas cake
156
white christmas
mud cakes 79
whole-spice syrup 212

conversion chart

MEASURES

One Australian metric measuring cup holds approximately 250ml, one Australian metric tablespoon holds 20ml, one Australian metric teaspoon holds 5ml.

The difference between one country's measuring cups and another's is within a two- or three-teaspoon variance, and will not affect your cooking results.North America, New Zealand and the United Kingdom use a 15ml tablespoon.

All cup and spoon measurements are level. The most accurate way of measuring dry ingredients is to weigh them. When measuring liquids, use a clear glass or plastic jug with the metric markings.

We use large eggs with an average weight of 60g.

LIQUID MEASURES

METRIC	IMPERIAL
30ml	1 fluid oz
60ml	2 fluid oz
100ml	3 fluid oz
125ml	4 fluid oz
150ml	5 fluid oz (¼ pint/1 gill)
190ml	6 fluid oz
250ml	8 fluid oz
300ml	10 fluid oz (½ pint)
500ml	16 fluid oz
600ml	20 fluid oz (1 pint)
1000ml (1 litre)	1¾ pints

LENGTH MEASURES

METRIC	IMPERIAL
3mm	⅛in
6mm	¼in
1cm	½in
2cm	¾in
2.5cm	1in
5cm	2in
6cm	2½in
8cm	3in
10cm	4in
13cm	5in
15cm	6in
18cm	7in
20cm	8in
23cm	9in
25cm	10in
28cm	11in
30cm	12in (1ft)

DRY MEASURES

METRIC	IMPERIAL
15g	½oz
30g	1oz
60g	2oz
90g	3oz
125g	4oz (¼lb)
155g	5oz
185g	6oz
220g	7oz
250g	8oz (½lb)
280g	9oz
315g	10oz
345g	11oz
375g	12oz (¾lb)
410g	13oz
440g	14oz
470g	15oz
500g	16oz (1lb)
750g	24oz (1½lb)
1kg	32oz (2lb)

OVEN TEMPERATURES

These oven temperatures are only a guide for conventional ovens.
For fan-forced ovens, check the manufacturer's manual.

	°C (CELSIUS)	°F (FAHRENHEIT)	GAS MARK
Very slow	120	250	½
Slow	150	275 – 300	1 – 2
Moderately slow	160	325	3
Moderate	180	350 – 375	4 – 5
Moderately hot	200	400	6
Hot	220	425 – 450	7 – 8
Very hot	240	475	9

Published in 2010 by ACP Books, Sydney

ACP Books are published by ACP Magazines, a division of PBL Media Pty Limited

ACP BOOKS

General manager Christine Whiston
Editor-in-chief Susan Tomnay
Creative director & designer Hieu Chi Nguyen
Art director Hannah Blackmore
Senior editor Stephanie Kistner
Food director Pamela Clark
Food editor Cathie Lonnie
Sales & rights director Brian Cearnes
Marketing manager Bridget Cody
Senior business analyst Rebecca Varela
Operations manager David Scotto
Production manager Victoria Jefferys

Published by ACP Books, a division of ACP Magazines Ltd.
54 Park St, Sydney NSW Australia 2000. GPO Box 4088, Sydney, NSW 2001.
Phone +61 2 9282 8618 Fax +61 2 9267 9438
acpbooks@acpmagazines.com.au www.acpbooks.com.au

Printed by Toppan Printing Co., China.

Australia Distributed by Network Services, GPO Box 4088, Sydney, NSW 2001.
Phone +61 2 9282 8777 Fax +61 2 9264 3278
networkweb@networkservicescompany.com.au

United Kingdom Distributed by Australian Consolidated Press (UK),
10 Scirocco Close, Moulton Park Office Village, Northampton, NN3 6AP.
Phone +44 1604 642 200 Fax +44 1604 642 300
books@acpuk.com www.acpuk.com

New Zealand Distributed by Southern Publishers Group, 21 Newton Road, Auckland.
Phone +64 9 360 0692 Fax +64 9 360 0695 hub@spg.co.nz

South Africa Distributed by PSD Promotions, 30 Diesel Road Isando, Gauteng Johannesburg.
PO Box 1175, Isando 1600, Gauteng Johannesburg.
Phone +27 11 392 6065/6/7 Fax +27 11 392 6079/80 orders@psdprom.co.za

Title: Cakes/food director Pamela Clark
ISBN: 978-1-74245-000-1 (pbk)
Notes: Includes index.
Subjects: Cake. Cookery.
Other authors/contributors: Clark, Pamela
Dewey number: 641.8653
© ACP Magazines Ltd 2010
ABN 18 053 273 546

To order books, phone 136 116 (within Australia) or **order online** at www.acpbooks.com.au
Send recipe enquiries to: recipeenquiries@acpmagazines.com.au

Front cover & additional photography Julie Crespel
Front cover & additional styling Kate Nixon
Front cover & additional food preparation Sharon Kennedy